Men Head East, Women Turn Right

How to Meet in the Middle
When Facing Change

Sabra E. Brock, M.S., and Joseph F. Dooley, Ph.D.

ADAMS MEDIA

AVON, MASSACHUSETTS

Copyright ©2004 Sabra E. Brock and Joseph F. Dooley. All rights reserved.
This book, or parts thereof, may not be reproduced in any form
without permission from the publisher; exceptions are made for
brief excerpts used in published reviews.

Published by
Adams Media, an F+W Publications Company
57 Littlefield Street, Avon, MA 02322. U.S.A.
www.adamsmedia.com

ISBN: 1-58062-806-0

Printed in Canada.

J I H G F E D C B A

Library of Congress Cataloging-in-Publication Data
Brock, Sabra E.
Men head east, women turn right / Sabra E. Brock and Joseph F. Dooley.
p.   cm.
ISBN 1-58062-806-0
1. Sex role. 2. Masculinity. 3. Femininity. 4. Social change.
I. Dooley, Joseph F. II. Title.
HQ1075.B75 2004
305.3--dc22

2003022943

This publication is designed to provide accurate and authoritative information with regard to the subject matter covered. It is sold with the understanding that the publisher is not engaged in rendering legal, accounting, or
other professional advice. If legal advice or other expert assistance is
required, the services of a competent professional person should be sought.
—From a *Declaration of Principles* jointly adopted by a Committee of the
American Bar Association and a Committee of Publishers and Associations

Many of the designations used by manufacturers and sellers to distinguish
their products are claimed as trademarks. Where those designations appear
in this book and Adams Media was aware of a trademark claim, the designations have been printed with initial capital letters.

This book is available at quantity discounts for bulk purchases.
For information, call 1-800-872-5627.

Contents

Acknowledgments

To Claire Gerus and Marshall Klein, our agents and editorial consultants, who expertly and supportively coached us through every one of the many steps that brought this book to publication; to Jill Alexander, our most favorite editor, whose many excellent suggestions and enthusiasm made every step easier; and to the whole staff at Adams Media for their ideas and support. And, of course, to the many people whose lives have been an inspiration to us.

Introduction

CHANGE IS EVERYWHERE! MOREOVER, WOMEN AND MEN HAVE different strategies for dealing with change. *Men Head East, Women Turn Right: How to Meet in the Middle When Facing Change* shows how this inevitable force can be harnessed to help you be happier and more successful. Patterns of change are predictable—whether the change is small or large, personal or universal, in your work life or your personal life. If you know how men and women are programmed to react, you'll be smarter when change happens.

Change will happen, that's a given; you need to find out how to make it work for you. You can do one of three things:

- Do nothing.
- Do more of the same (with more effort this time).
- Change how you approach things.

This book shows how to handle changes to be happier and more productive. By understanding the opposite gender's change management approach, you can work together more effectively. It's not just that men and women are opposites; there's also the matter of patterning. Men and women approach the world very differently. Knowing what the differences are can help you resolve and prevent conflict.

Change involves moving in a different direction. This could be a literal change, such as moving to a new city or beginning a new job. Or it could mean a shift in attitude about a particular situation. The metaphor "Men head east, women turn right" for which this book is titled expresses how men and women perceive directions differently. Studies have shown that when a woman needs directions on how to get to a destination, she tends to look for visual cues that are a part of her familiar environment. She looks for landmarks that are easily recognizable and that have immediate relevance for her. Thus, a woman is more likely to think of getting from point A to point B in terms of making a right at the gas station, driving for approximately ten minutes, and making a turn at the green house on the left. Men, on the other hand, tend to be more detached and abstract about their environment. A man will think about the exact same directions as heading east at the gas station, going 1.5 miles, and turning north onto Main Street.

When a woman turns her car right and a man turns his east, they are going in the exact same direction, but their perceptions about the situation may be miles apart. Neither approach is right or wrong; as you'll discover in this book, each one has its inherent strengths. But when a man tries to direct a woman with "male" signals, or a woman guides a man with "female" signs, confusion can ensue.

When change happens, men take action; women reach out and innovate.

Some situations in a relationship work effortlessly. But at other times, the very same people can become lost and confused without a clue as to why. This book helps people in relationships overcome those difficulties by helping them learn how to meet in the middle.

The Structure of This Book

Men Head East, Women Turn Right gives you the resources to deal with the profound changes in work life and in personal relationships. The Brock Method, described within, improves the way you manage change in relationships with all the important people in your life by helping you do the following:

- Learn your natural strengths as a man or woman dealing with change
- Understand how the opposite gender usually handles change
- Improve the way you work with others in your life, your partner, your family, and coworkers during change
- Get exposure to specific examples of how people like you have coped with change successfully

This book also answers these questions:

- How do men and women approach change differently?
- What are the three steps we all need to go through in reacting to change? How are men and women likely to handle each one?
- What are the five skills for making change work? Which are easiest for women? Which are easiest for men?
- How do men and women approach the eight major life changes?
- What can we learn from each other?
- Why aren't we communicating?

The book also includes quizzes to find out your natural change management style and other tools to help you explore your strengths and strategies in handling change.

Men Head East, Women Turn Right is a guidebook for successful relationships in the twenty-first century, a time guaranteed to be full of change. It reveals how men and women approach change very differently and how they each use what works well for them. It's essential to understand how the other gender approaches change in order to create more successful relationships in life.

Expanding our understanding of how the opposite sex deals with change helps avoid misunderstanding in relationships. If you remember that your partner or parent or friend can find successful, though different, approaches to change, all your relationships will improve.

Think of this book as a practical tool kit for managing your life. We've devoted an entire chapter to how men and women approach change differently in each of the eight major life areas. You'll come away better able to handle change in every aspect of your life. We'll help you approach changes in romance, career, and all the other vital aspects of your life.

The book is divided into five sections. Part I sets up the differences in the male and female approach to change. Part II considers how men and women can work through the three steps of change by making use of the five change skills of the Brock Method. Part III considers how men and women approach change in the relationship parts of their lives: marriage and divorce, dating, parenting, and managing elderly parents. The chapters in Part IV cover changes in location, health, and financial situations.

You'll be smarter about change in every part of your life.

In Part V, we show how the male and female approaches to change are different in the workplace and the world, and how the timing of changes for men and women creates distinct challenges.

PART I

Women, Men, and Change

The first chapter of *Men Head East, Women Turn Right* describes how over time, the need for tools to deal with change grows ever more important. Chapter 2 lays out the scientific basis for the different ways men and women approach change, and Chapter 3 defines the eight major life changes where these differences are apparent. In Chapter 4, we'll help you to define your own change style.

Chapter 1

Your Tool Kit for Making Change Work

EACH AND EVERY DAY PEOPLE ALL OVER THE WORLD PICK UP newspapers or tune in to the nightly news to see reports of exciting new developments in science, medicine, technology, and business. We all feel as if we are living in a brand-new world, a world that is filled to overflowing with new gadgets, new rules, and new opportunities.

These changes are coming at us with ever-increasing speed. For thousands of years our forebears lived traditional lives, where the emphasis was on doing things much as their predecessors had done before them. The template for successful living was simply to do what had worked before. Rules of life were worked out over the generations by trial and error. Sticking to familiar ways of doing things ensured success for the family and the tribe. Our traditions, our beliefs, our bodies, and even our minds have been adapted to this very practical way of doing things.

Men are conditioned by biology and culture to seek action. Millions of years ago, early humans evolved and organized themselves so that men hunted and women tended the home fires. Men were on the average larger, more muscular, stronger, and faster. As times went on, the most action-oriented men were selected out as the best hunters. Nature rewarded males who liked to take immediate action.

By contrast, females stayed at camp tending the children, keeping the fires going, and gathering plants and vegetables. All of these activities were vital for the success of the tribe. Nature selected females who could cooperate.

But now, at the beginning of the twenty-first century, change comes hurtling at us with the speed of light. The telephone connects us to each other and to new information in a way totally unknown by the thousands of generations of human beings who preceded us on this earth. But that's not enough for us today. The phones must have speed dialing. They must be cellular so that we can carry them in our pockets. They must be digital and connected to the Internet, then have faster modems, then be tiny, then be on our wrists.

Technology isn't the only culprit here. The environment in which we earn our living is changing quickly too. Twenty years ago, most people in the United States were perfectly content to settle down into a long-term job with a big company. It was secure. You could count on a job and a paycheck to support your family. That's not true anymore. Recently, downsizing has become the buzzword in American industry, with companies firing people in record numbers. No job is secure anymore. Whether you are the big boss or the lowest clerk, you could lose your job and your paycheck overnight without warning.

And the family you are worried about supporting? Well, unfortunately that has changed too. Now divorce hits one out of two marriages. Single adult families, second families, and Brady Bunch families (three of hers and three of his) are the rule in America, not the exception. What was once the refuge from the world is now the most glaring reminder in our lives of how deeply and permanently things change.

The most profound change has come in the role of the two genders. Women now are a major force in the workplace and are making serious inroads in middle and upper management. In today's organizations, the senior person may very well be female and the support person male. We have to learn new ways of relating to each other—not just to avoid sexual harassment charges, but also to be able to capitalize on the natural strengths of each gender. How can a female boss bring out the best in her male subordinates? How do we manage in a dual-gender work force when change is so much a constant?

Within the family, roles have been dramatically altered. We can no longer assume that a U.S. household will have two parents, one male and one female. Now Mom is most likely to be away from the home during the day; the children may stay at a day-care facility while she works late or has a drink with a date after work. Or the parent at home may be a mister and not a missus.

We've done original research on how men and women approach change differently. All of the principles in this book have been tried and tested. Each gender has coping strategies that come more naturally to them and appear very strange to the opposite sex. Knowing how men and women approach the eight types of life change can help reduce stress and clear the way for personal growth.

Tools for Change

What are the new tools available for making change work? Three types of tools are now available to us. First, our research shows that an understanding of the different ways men and women manage change helps us communicate and use each other's skills to approach change situations more productively and happily.

The male approach to change is more inward, focused, and structured.

Second, there is the concept of the three steps of adjusting to change. William Bridges first introduced this in his book *Managing Transitions: Making the Most of Change in Your Life.* Remembering to observe each one clears the way for moving on to the next day. We've found that men and women have different ways to handle each step.

The Three Change Steps

1. Say goodbye.

2. Move through the Middles.

3. Start a new beginning.

Third, there are five important skills for adapting to new situations. In a study of hundreds of thousands of Peace Corps volunteers, with the goal of understanding why some volunteers were successful in adapting to new situations while others opted out, the following five skills were found to be essential to successfully managing transition:

- Creating a personal vision
- Reframing
- Having emotional resilience
- Being flexible
- Having a strong sense of self

The Brock Method is a way to increase your skill-set for dealing with change in each of these five vital areas. It was devised to aid people in coping with change of all types with wisdom we've gained from our years of researching and teaching change as a personal growth stimulus.

Men and women exhibit these five skills in very different ways. For example, we talked with Hank, one of the hundreds of people in our research on how men and women manage change. When he figured that he was about to be let go after three rounds of layoffs at his dot-com employer, he first blamed his employer for not running the company right. Then he pulled himself together and looked for new opportunities. He demonstrated flexibility in response to a major change in his life.

The female structure for change reaches out for counsel and support.

Ruth, at the same dot-com, reacted by blaming herself and agonizing over how she could have prevented it. She then called her best friend Sally to talk about it, even though Sally didn't know anything about dot-coms. Then she got on the Web to see what the growth areas were for jobs in her community. Ruth, like Hank, expressed flexibility, though in a feminine way.

The male approach to change is likely to be more inward and focused, as well as dependent on a traditional structure. The female strategy, on the other hand, is to reach out for counsel and support. The woman is likely to have a less structured view of how change impacts her life.

Making Change Work for You

After years of teaching and research, we have found that each of the changes in life that we encounter almost every week can be handled in a way that allows us to make change work for us, instead of against us.

Have you ever found yourself in the middle of some big change in life, such as getting married, when you suddenly realized that things were really different, and you thought, "How do I get through this?" We've found that most people feel this way when in a change of life, be it marriage, dating, or becoming a parent or a grandparent. People realize that circumstances in life have made things different, and they wonder how they can handle the change for the good.

The truth is that when you are in such a state, the best thing to do is recognize the three steps of change and then to apply the five elements of the Brock Method to increase your chances of making change work successfully.

The Brock Method for Increasing Your Change Skills

Create a personal vision.

Reframe.

Build emotional resilience.

Practice your flexibility.

Increase your self-sense.

Chapter 2

The Basis for Differences Between Men and Women

THERE'S BEEN MUCH DISCUSSION ABOUT WHETHER THE DIFFERENT female and male reactions to change (along with many other gender differences) are just a result of our cultural environment. Are the genders born as "blank slates," and are differences created by what society expects? It is very true that the upbringing of boys and girls affects the way each gender reacts to change. However, what we see with men and women is that there's simply a difference in our brains. Convincing evidence exists to suggest that there's a wiring specific to each gender that predisposes men and women to react differently to change.

Our Genetic Program

All men and women exist in, and are part of, nature. It is not surprising to us at the beginning of the twenty-first century that the human body and its life functions are controlled and regulated by DNA located within the nucleus of each of trillions of cells in our bodies. We also know that DNA is organized in groups called genes and in longer strings called chromosomes. This DNA is distributed into gene clusters that we inherit at conception from our parents. The genes that we receive at the beginning of life are responsible for controlling, determining, and, in a profound way, creating all of the millions of cellular connections, hormonal communications, neurochemical nerve firings, and all other biochemical processes in our bodies from birth until the day we die.

For us, DNA and its genetic packets control what it is to be human. It's just as true that DNA controls what it means to be a house cat, a lion, or a chimpanzee. In fact, it turns out that very small differences in DNA composition and activation within the genes make very large differences in physical appearance and behavior, even in two very closely related animals.

For example, the DNA of chimpanzees differs from another closely related primate species, the bonobo, by less than 1 percent. But this small difference in DNA results in enormous differences in size and behavior of this advanced species. In general, zoologists have reported that chimpanzees are frequently aggressive, excessively territorial, male dominated, sexually predatory, and capable of male coalition violence. On the other hand, bonobos are smaller animals that use sexual activity for social communication. They are generally peaceable, and their social structure is female hierarchical. In other words, the differences in DNA in the genes makes for wiring differences in the brain, and probably for different concentrations of neurotransmitters at the nerve synapses, ultimately determining behavioral differences.

> DNA controls what it means to be human, as much as it controls what it means to be any other animal.

The DNA and gene differences in chimpanzees and bonobos do not make one species better than the other. The two are simply different. They naturally respond in very different ways to the same environmental stimulus. Each is equally effective, but they are different. In other words, each type of primate uses the skills best suited to its survival. Millions of years of evolution have shaped the responses of the two animal groups to hunger, sexual reproduction, the need for communication, and all of the other exigencies of survival. And they are both still here for us to write about. This is a good indication that nature has found both of their group approaches valid and useful for survival.

Mental and Physical Connections

The mental world is shaped and guided by DNA and genetic information contained in the nucleus of the cells. Behavioral traits like anger, sexual desire, will to live, and many others are evolutionary responses of human beings that are implemented by the circuitry of the brain.

The mental world is grounded in the physical. Do house cats pick up human language as quickly as human children? Of course not. Anybody who keeps a cat as a pet knows that while cats are very advanced animals—intelligent and clever, with an unnerving knack for getting their own way—they do not learn language as easily as human babies do.

Communication in humans is structured very differently than in other mammals such as cats. The DNA that is specific to humans and its genetic arrangement has determined in advance that human babies can learn language very well in three years just by listening. Cats are programmed very well for different things that human babies (or adults, for that matter) can't easily do, like jumping up to five times their height or hunting small animals.

The point here is that there are many physical and behavioral traits that are programmed into our genes at the moment of conception. Some of these differences are easily understood, like the blue eyes you inherited from your mother or the height you got from your father. You might even inherit a tendency to a disease, like cancer or diabetes, or other characteristics, like the ability to play musical instruments or a tendency to be humorous, introspective, or gregarious.

These traits are instilled at conception. The genetic programming of brain development controls other more complex funtions of the brain such as hemisphere size and capillary blood flow. These vital elements of brain function typically appear very early in life, in the first critical synthesis of brain tissue and subsequent hormonal and environmental stimuli, both *in utero* and after birth. It turns out that thoughts and feelings, joys and fears, and all of an individual's emotional life are the sum of the physical form and biochemical function of the brain.

There is more. Medical science has recently been able to watch the living brain in action. Using radiolabels and magnetic resonance instruments (MRI), scientists have found that many of the specific regions of the brain are activated in different emotional or mental states. This finding makes sense and is consistent with the anatomical diversity of the brain. Just as other parts of your body are specialized for different functions, like the kidneys or the stomach, your brain has specialized parts too. Show a person a bright light, and one or more parts of his brain become more active. Make a sound, and other parts respond. If he talks, still other parts of his brain respond. If he is fearful, or angry, or feeling sexy, different parts of the brain will light up.

Men and women are wired differently.

It has also been found that the brains of men and women are wired differently and that they respond to stimulus in a profoundly different manner. For example, males on average have larger brains per unit of body weight than females. But female brains frequently distribute active parts differently when, for example, a woman is speaking. The sites activated in the female brain involved with speech are distributed more broadly in both hemispheres of the brain. In the male brain, on the other hand, speech centers are much more localized in the left hemisphere.

Is one better than the other? Probably not, at least in our time. Evolutionary psychology leaves plenty of room for speculation on the survival benefits of male and female brain arrangements. Suffice it to say that in our ancestors, living as they did in the wild, successful adaptation based on gender roles was probably a good strategy for survival. We do not know for certain, but it seems to make sense that the very human style of communication between group members using speech was heavily selected according to work style. It's not surprising that female group members needed to talk to each other in a very different way than male group members. The assumption here is that female group members were heavily involved in food gathering, child rearing, and fire making, and the male members were occupied with hunting and catching food, making weapons and tools and protecting the group from outside threats.

The human experience seems to be grounded in duality. Our bodies have two arms, two legs, two kidneys, two lungs, two eyes, and two ears. We also seem to have two types of brain structures, as well as two sexes. There is even a duality in our physical and spiritual nature. Men and women look different. We are built differently, function differently physically— men in general are bigger and stronger, while women can have babies—and we use different parts of the brain to talk and worry and fear. We are all human, but we are different from one another. It is important for good communication that we recognize and explore our differences so that knowledge of the differences becomes another one of our strengths.

How Men and Women Go Through the Three Steps of Change

Both men and women have inborn strengths for coping with change and getting through the three essential change steps. Each gender has effective ways of handling change. They're just different.

Through our research, we explored the places where the feminine inclination is stronger and where men more easily use their skills. We talked with several hundred men and women about how they reacted to change and how they saw the opposite sex coping. This is what we found.

Men tend to find the process of reframing a foreign one. Also unlike their female counterparts, men find it difficult to express their emotions. They are not naturally gifted in resilience or flexibility.

Women are structured with more of a connection between the right and left sides of their brains. This means that women connect the right side, or talking part, of the brain more with the left, the action part. Men find it easier to act without much talking; women need to talk with others before committing to action.

This means that women find it easier to talk with others and to take the time to say the necessary goodbyes to anything that they may be leaving behind. Without going through this first step, *Say Goodbye,* human beings never fully adapt to change.

Women Handle Change By . . .	Men Handle Change By . . .
Reaching out, talking, researching ways change can happen.	Taking action.
Taking time to say goodbye (may get stuck in the Middles).	Skipping goodbye and taking control to move through the Middles.
Building slowly to a new beginning.	Moving fast into a new beginning (once committed).
Visualizing the future in words and images.	Setting an example rather than explaining themselves.
Taking to reframing, once explained.	Coming more naturally to a sense of self-confidence.
Expressing emotions and finding it easier to be emotionally resilient and flexible.	
Finding a need to strengthen self-sense (usually).	

The second step of change, *Get Through the Middles*, requires taking control and getting through an awkward period fast. Men find this easier because their brains are set up so they don't dwell on the emotional part of change but just do what's necessary.

Women tend to accomplish the last step of change, *Start a New Beginning*, through visualizing the future and then expressing that vision to others. Men, again, rely on action and hard work to set an example that others can follow. It can be a surprise to a man to look back and find that no one's behind him.

Women find it easier to address their emotions and develop the emotional resilience that change requires. They also are open to more unstructured solutions and can be flexible when it comes to trying them out.

Our data show that compared to men, women are weakest in terms of their sense of self. Almost always, if a woman can strengthen her confidence in herself, she will weather change more effectively.

Mistakes Women Make During Change	Men Think . . .
Taking too long to talk about change before acting.	She's procrastinating.
Getting stuck thinking out options.	She's weak and inflexible.
Talking about the future in detail.	This is not relevant to what's needed now.
Spending time grieving for what's lost.	She's too emotional. Get on with it.
Forgetting to think about themselves and their needs.	If she wants something, she'll tell me.
Taking time to look at things in new ways and seeing many options.	She's indecisive. Why doesn't she just pick one and do it?

Mistakes Men Make During Change	Women Think . . .
Forgetting to identify or say goodbye to what they're losing in the change.	Men have no feelings.
Acting without considering consequences.	He's rash.
Acting without talking and then expecting others to follow.	Where did he go?
Taking the first action they think of.	Why doesn't he think things through?
Expecting to try again if first action fails.	Why not think first?

Learning Change

Here are some points learned through our research that can help men and women improve their reactions to the other gender during times of change.

He Needs to Remember That . . .

She needs time to grieve and talk about the losses that change brings.

She can get stuck in thinking through what to do in times of change.

She may forget to think about her own needs in helping others during change.

She thinks of the future graphically.

It's easier for her to be creative during times of change.

He Needs Not To . . .

Say, "Everything will be fine. What are you worrying about?"

Act without telling her why or listening to her reactions.

Think she'll speak up if she needs something.

Expect her to follow your lead without talking with her first.

Ignore her solutions.

She Needs to Remember That . . .

When change happens, men need to take action.

If she needs support, she should ask for it.

Sometimes it's better to follow his lead first and then ask for the reasons later.

Just because he's doing several things at the same time doesn't mean he's not listening to you.

He isn't used to looking at the person he's talking with all the time.

She Needs Not To . . .

Think he's insensitive.

Assume he knows what she needs.

Tell him he's wrong to take immediate action during times of change.

Expect him to spend much time talking with friends during a big change.

Take it personally when he looks away during an important conversation.

Chapter 3

Making Change Work:
How Women Do It; How Men Do It

DIFFERENCES CAN BRING MISUNDERSTANDING AND CONFLICT. They can also bring growth, enrichment, and better ways to make change work in your life. Once you know how the opposite gender is likely to approach change, you're better equipped to deal with it. The ideas in this book will change your approach to romance, dating, courtship, marriage, and divorce. You'll see all your relationships more clearly: those with friends, your family, and people in the workplace. And you'll think of the inevitable changes in finances, health, and the world in a new fresh light.

This chapter presents stories about how men and women use a wide variety of different approaches to deal with change in marriage, job, romance, parenting, health, and the other areas of their lives. We will see that men and women use very different methods for coping with changes in their lives. Both genders usually succeed in finding ways that work very well for them. It turns out that men and women alike all have natural inborn strengths from which to draw. We will explore why this is and the value our differing strengths lend to every-day home and work life.

We don't mean to say that all men act one way all the time, anymore than we would claim that all women behave in the same way in response to change. As we grow up and acquire wisdom, we can borrow from the opposite gender's style to give us more strength in each situation. However, doing what comes naturally uses less energy and is less stressful.

When considering the different approaches men and women take to change, there are a few especially important points to keep in mind:

1. Each gender has a natural style that is more comfortable for them when approaching change.
2. Women are more likely to reach out for help, research options, and handle change in a less structured way.
3. Men tend to take action and are more comfortable with traditional solutions and structures.
4. It's fine to borrow, but constantly working against your grain is stressful.
5. Knowing your natural style as well as the other gender's makes it easier to understand and communicate with the opposite sex.

Why Women and Men Approach Change Differently

New brain research proves the female and male brains are different. Women have a thicker connector between the right and left hemispheres. The two genders also process three activities in different places in the brain, as follows:

- *Language:* Women process language only in the front of the left hemisphere; men process it in both the front and the back.
- *Visual-spatial perception:* Men use only the right hemisphere, whereas women use both brain hemispheres.
- *Emotions:* Men's emotional responses are concentrated in the right hemisphere; women's are spread between both.

When a function is more highly concentrated in one area of the brain, it can be accomplished with less interference. Brain researchers conclude that the concentration of these functions makes language easier for women. Men, on the other hand, have better brain structures for visual-spatial performance.

In addition, women secrete oxytoxin at time of stress. This, combined with sex-linked hormones like estrogen, conditions them to be more reliant on social networks and more nurturing under stress. Men's testosterone engenders a competitive reaction (fight or flight).

Biology translates to behavior. Girls speak at an earlier point in their development than boys do. Women are generally better at language than men and have more sensitive hearing. Most men test higher on visual-spatial ability than most women. Folklore has it that most men are better at figuring out directions, even without asking. Actually, there's even documented research to prove that. Men in general have a greater ability to visualize abstractly; this is one reason that, as in our title, men often will "head east" when following directions. A woman is more

> If you know how your partner approaches change, you'll both do a better job together.

likely to rely on concrete visual landmarks ("turn left at the brick church") in order to reach the same destination.

Furthermore, because women process visual-spatial tasks in both hemispheres, it's harder for a woman to talk about what she's doing when she's doing it. That's why a man will continue to do things when listening rather than give a speaker his undivided attention.

Because of the way their brains function, with emotions being processed in both hemispheres, most women find it easier to talk about emotions, their own and others. Men have an underlying brain structure that makes it harder for them to talk about emotions.

Women do remember emotional events longer than men, giving credence to the observation that wives ruminate over marital spats whereas husbands tend to forget them.

How History Has Reinforced Biological Gender Differences

Certain ways of dealing with change are more natural for women, and some are more natural for men. Our explanation goes back to prehistoric times. We all got to where we are today because our ancestors were able to work together to meet the challenges of evolution.

We think that much of the difference in handling change goes back to early human history. Men were charged with the hunting and had to focus single-mindedly on that activity so that the tribe could eat. Therefore, men required a process that didn't necessitate thinking, where roles were clear, and that facilitated immediate action.

Women, on the other hand, had the task of gathering. At the same time they were responsible for child care and home maintenance. It's easy to see how different approaches to managing change evolved in our ancestors. Woman needed to be more patient and to be able to focus on several things at one time. Women had to be more emotional to be sensitive to the needs of their children. They had to use language more sensitively to reinforce the protection of the group for their families.

That's the background behind Margaret, a professional trainer, and her statement in our change research. Margaret said, "Women are more willing to ask for help. Women are more willing to explore their feelings about the change. Men want to

> Men instinctively are warriors; women are gatherers.

'fix it' fast. Women are more flexible. It's harder for men to admit that their approach is not the best." Men were trained to be warriors. Therefore, once an approach was decided, it was better for the tribe to stay with the chosen strategy.

It's Okay to Celebrate Our Differences

It has been politically incorrect in recent decades to say that men and women are fundamentally different in their skills. However, we have noticed in our own lives that our reactions to change were very different, the man's from the woman's. But each of us had an effective way to deal with most changes. We just didn't understand each other's approach to change.

We decided to study the differences in the male and female approaches to change. What we found has changed our lives, and it will change your life too. To cope with our new world, it's essential that you learn how men and women handle the three essential steps of change and how they exhibit the five change skills.

Whether we're younger or older, most of us say there's been a lot of change in our lives. As we talked with people who ranged in age from their twenties to their eighties, we found that most people feel the pressure of change. Many of us even welcome it, finding new ways to do things.

The thing we found was important was to recognize the necessity of going with what worked for each of us, rather than trying to conform to the "approved" way. The more we knew our innate strategies for managing change, the more we could understand each other, communicate, and, where necessary, make an effort to borrow from the other gender's natural style—even if it would take a little more energy. However, if you have a larger tool kit to draw from, you can cope successfully more of the time. Our goal for this book is to help you do the same thing.

Let's take Jill, for instance. Jill gets very annoyed when she's overcharged at a restaurant. She takes it personally, and her annoyance can escalate the situation into an argument. But the same scenario doesn't bother her partner, Hugh. He handles it calmly and gets the problem solved. When they're out together, he takes care of any problems with the bill. So when Jill is by herself and she's overcharged, she remembers Hugh's calm approach to talking with the offending waiter. She borrows that approach. The problem gets solved with no arguments and less frustration on Jill's part.

How We're Different

Ask yourself these important questions about dealing with change. After you decide on your own answers, read the following section (no peeking!) to see how your responses compare with those of the hundreds of men and women in our survey on managing change. There are no right or wrong answers, and your feelings about change won't necessarily follow those of our survey participants. Each person has an individual change style, and its elements won't always fall on strict gender lines.

1. Do you think men and women manage change differently?

_____

_____

_____

2. In what ways are they different?

_____

_____

_____

3. How much change have you had in your life so far?

_____

_____

_____

4. What's your attitude toward change?

_____

_____

_____

5. Which do you value more: tradition or innovation?

_____

_____

_____

6. What's your usual strategy for managing change?

_____

_____

_____

_____

And now for the answers that we found most common in our survey:

Q. Do you think men and women manage change differently?
A. Most people, about two-thirds of those we talked with, said yes, the two genders are different in their approaches to change. About half the men in the sample said they observed a difference, whereas a majority of the women believed there was a gender difference in facing change.

Q. In what ways are they different?
A. Men and women had different perspectives. Most women thought men were more resistant to change; women also thought that men like to fix it fast. Women believed that men may internalize the impact of change, but then don't like to be introspective and think about their reactions to it. Men thought women manage change more emotionally and ask for help more often. Women said, about themselves, that they approach change in a less structured way, and do more analysis than most men.

Q. How much change have you had in your life so far?
A. Most women and men thought they've had a lot of change. Very few said not too much change has occurred so far in their lives. There was no difference between men and women here.

Q. What's your attitude toward change?
A. Most people saw change as inevitable, consistent with having seen a lot of it in their lives. One-third welcomed it. A small minority hated it.

Q. Which do you value more: tradition or innovation?

A. Most people said it depended on the situation, but many were likely to be innovative in approaching change. Men were a little more likely to indicate that they stayed with success. Women valued innovation more than men.

Q. What's your usual strategy for managing change?

A. Almost everybody reported learning new ways of doing things. Women were more likely to ask for support, complain, and watch others. Men were more likely to ask directly to be able to cope with the new circumstances.

The Eight Major Life Changes

Kind of Change	Examples of Bigger Changes	Examples of Smaller Changes
Marital status	Married	Spouse takes a sabbatical
	Divorced	Spouse's work schedule changed from days to nights
Dating and courtship	New relationship	Business travel takes one partner out of town
	Breakup	Getting engaged
Children and parents	Empty nest	Child starts school
	Birth/adoption	Child takes up new hobby
	Deterioration of parents' health	Parents retire
	Death of parent	Parent remarries
Location	Relocated to an unfamiliar community	New neighbors
Health	Heart attack	Sprained ankle
	Cancer diagnosis	Need a mammogram
	Major accident	
Financial	Loss of salary	Cost-of-living raise
	Windfall	
Job/workplace	Laid off	Moved from cubicle to office
	Retired	Assigned smaller territory
	Returned to work force	
External	Attack on United States	Commuting path changed
	War	Change in ruling political party

For each major life change, there's a male strategy and a female strategy. For example, when two parents are faced with an empty nest, the mother is more likely to engage grown children in the network of family activities, like a grandmother's birthday or a christening for a new grandchild. Men, however, lean more toward helping grown children solve their life issues: what to do when they're laid off by a dot-com or how to network when relocated. In becoming a caretaker for elderly parents, a woman's strategy is to bring them into the home, under her care. The male strategy is to find a team of caregivers to provide the parents with support.

Now we'll give you highlights from the stories of the people we've worked with who are going through each of the eight major life changes.

Marriage and Divorce

We have observed that men and women in both happy and unhappy marriages approach change in different ways. Knowing that your partner's different approach to change is natural can help a couple through a stressful situation. In our research we talked with two couples about how they adapted to the changes that marriage brings. Deborah and Mike and Angela and Byron were two couples starting out at the same place. Although they lived in different parts of the country, they had a lot in common, including their youth and the fact that it was a first marriage for both couples.

While Deborah and Mike found that they were able to penetrate the differences in the way each approached change, Angela and Byron couldn't. Both wives were hurt by their new husbands' inability to talk about the daily emotions of life. Both asked, "Is it because he doesn't love me? Even when he will talk, he has one hand on the remote. He thinks he's listening because he's put the television on mute."

Similarly, both husbands were perplexed by their wives' lack of understanding that they were trying to help the marriage by doing things differently in order to please them. They started to be jealous of the time the women spent on the phone chatting with family and friends about the new things happening to them.

Each little change that came up was a mountain to climb. As change piled more and more stress on each marriage, Deborah and Mike were impelled to solve their problems. Angela and Byron, on the other hand, didn't find out about the different male and female reactions to change until after they had divorced. What made the difference between the two couples? Deborah and Mike recognized that there is a male way and a female way to approach the changes of marriage. Understanding each other's approach helped them forge a common path.

Angela and Byron, however, ignored the different approaches to change that men and women have. "What in the world," Byron asked, "does change have to do with a relationship?" This might be the attitude of too many men. As Clara, a successful wife, observes, ". . . men generally prefer to remain in unhappy relationships and 'make the best of it' (perhaps finding gratification elsewhere), rather than seeking counseling/divorce." It's women who initiate the divorce 60 percent of the time.

We'll find out more in Chapter 9 about these two couples and effective ways of handling the changes that come with marriage and divorce.

Dating and Courtship

Through the changes that occur in dating and courtship, we found that women are more likely than men to consult others about the relationship, look for support from friends, or seek advice before taking action. It is important that men see this as an effective and quite natural female reaction to change, rather than a hesitation that can be viewed as a sign of weakness and doubt. When a man understands that his date or fiancée frequently reacts to change

Will David and Celeste ever get together?

in a very different way than he does—while still getting through it successfully, in her own way—a stronger relationship can develop between them. Chapter 10 details the ways men and women handle the changes of dating and courtship.

Before David understood the female approach, he was perplexed that Celeste wanted him to start spending weekends with her at her country home. It turns out that this was what her friends had advised. Everyone wanted to meet her new boyfriend. Celeste believed that living together on weekends would be a good way to find out if she and David were compatible. But David liked his apartment in the city, and he didn't want to give up his weekend sports get-togethers with his friends.

David realized that this was the way Celeste, as a woman, was programmed to approach change. On that basis, he agreed to try the arrangement out one weekend a month. However, he also asked that she spend one weekend in the city, so that they could be together and he could also see his friends.

Family Life

Family life is a predictable cycle of change, starting with birth and the establishment of relationships with parents and siblings, followed by the young adult's creation of a new home. Men and women are programmed by our brains and our culture to react to these changes in different ways. The more you know about what's natural for you and for the opposite sex, the better you'll be able to navigate the change challenges of children, parents, and the rest of your family.

In general, women are better at coping with changes in family situations. Suzanne, a mother and the wife of an executive of a high-tech company, puts it this way: "Men are more likely to plow through business changes and crumple at personal changes. Women tend to have more personal changes, which affect personal as well as professional aspects of life. Women will naturally reach out to find all the options in caring for family members." When her husband's job moved the family to Boise, Idaho, Suzanne reframed her disappointment over the loss of her interesting job and a fulfilling school for her daughter. In Boise, she became a leader in a program to create an alternate school for gifted children. She loves it because she's able to spend more time with her daughter.

How can Suzanne and Joy best use their natural approaches to meet the change challenges of growing children and aging parents?

Joy agrees, looking at her life as wife, mother, and secretary in the publishing world: "Women must be sufficiently flexible to play many roles—wife, mother, homemaker, and now, for many, employee. Because their daily life requires adjustments to multilevel situations, they grow in their ability to adapt to change." When her elderly mother needed full-time care, Joy changed her job to set up a word-processing business in her home, and asked her mother to come live in her house. A man would have been more likely to find an alternate care arrangement for an aging parent and then to work harder to fund the arrangement.

Read more about the ways men and women manage the changes that parenting brings in Chapter 11.

Moving

The changes involved with moving bring out different strengths and weakness in the male and female approach to change. Men are more comfortable when the move is structured. They prefer to simply make the decision and not to have to talk about the details much. Women, on the other hand, like to have time to think through what their lifestyle is going to be in the new situation. They're more open to the creative possibilities and will take time to find them.

Men are not as imaginative as women when it comes to realistically visualizing (rather than fantasizing) ways in which their lives could improve. In addition, they are less willing to deal with the details that change almost always requires. Men, in general, are more interested in financial stability, less trusting of intuition and emotion, and not as motivated by personal growth.

Take the example of Marcus and Hannah, who were shopping for a house. As Marcus told us, "I look at the structure of the place, what kind of heating does it have, does it have solar panels. Hannah is down on her hands and knees looking to see if there's hardwood floor under the ratty carpeting. She's also the one who can visualize adding a second story so we could have a view of the water. We see the property from entirely different viewpoints, so we've learned to compare notes immediately after we leave the realtor."

Health

When faced with the need to make a change because of medical advice, men prefer action. Alternately, they may go to the opposite extreme and choose not even to hear the advice. If a doctor says to lose weight because of high blood pressure, men will most likely head to the gym. It's a visible and positive action that can bring fast results. Women will do this too, but they are also more likely to turn to diet and other, subtler lifestyle changes.

Janet has had to face breast cancer. "Men hold it in; women share verbally and emotionally. Women are less afraid to face the reality of change—both its hardships and challenges. Men don't wait for someone to help them. Women often spend more time analyzing before changing." In addition, Janet says, "Women will ask for more help." When she got her diagnosis, she turned to a support group.

Find out more about the differences in the ways men and women manage health changes in Chapter 13.

Finances

Women need to understand that what might appear in a man to be resistance to change might actually be the calm before the storm as he prepares to go into action. Men need to value a woman's more analytic approach, even though it can look like procrastination to them.

Ellen, a financial counselor, observes that men and women react differently to changes in their financial picture. "Women are mentally more prepared and open to change. Men fear change inasmuch as it will force them to be more emotionally open and involved. Men can seem to resist and fight change. I see it in how they react to my recommendations for new investment strategies."

What are Ellen's female secrets to managing money for a largely male client base?

Ellen went on to say, "When change happens suddenly, like a drop in the stock market, men seem to take it more in stride and act quickly. Men are more objective and can adapt to change easier than women. Women tend to have an emotional attachment to certain situations. Women seem tied up in the details of the change. They see the path and plot the change, while men see the end of the path and 'just go for it.'"

Men do indeed "just go for it." This is a normal and usually quite healthy male-oriented response. Women can take a lesson from this tendency to move to direct action. Although it may not be her cup of tea, a woman can realize that the man in her life is following his natural inclination. One thing that helps people of both genders live with each other in harmony is understanding. Each gender reacts to change in entirely different ways, but both usually choose the response that works for them.

Turn to Chapter 14 for more about how men and women approach changes in their financial condition.

The Workplace

Our jobs are being dramatically affected by changes, such as new technology, layoffs, and the flattening of hierarchical organizations into teams. In the twenty-first century, many of us may work from home. We may have several careers, and we may find ourselves being forced to be more entrepreneurial. Women have an easier time taking advantage of the turbulent workplace because they are less invested in the traditional work structure.

It's easier to see the difference in work situations more clearly. At the office, we frequently hear statements such as, "Women are more intuitive and respond better to change. Women are also more inclined to actually seek out opportunities to change. They are more curious, risk-taking, and they tend to work together to effect change. Men use more hierarchy."

Richard, a private banking officer at a large brokerage firm, says, "In business I have witnessed many strong women who accept changes, think through the ramifications and simply go about dealing with the 'new.' Many men seem more afraid of change, less willing to learn new ideas, and much more resistant." He works for a company that for the past century has been dominated by men who have built a successful hierarchy and process. It is only now, with the more rapid pace of change, that male dominance is being challenged.

Men are generally better at coping with change in the workplace. Most organizations are set up in the hierarchical fashion that men prefer, and most organizations have built-in mechanisms for facing change. Men are particularly well suited to the old system of staying with one organization for a career and then retiring at sixty-five.

Women who entered the workplace twenty or thirty years ago had to use the male change-management strategy of fast definitive action in order to succeed. However, as the workplace becomes more fluid and organizations more team-based, female change management strategies are becoming more effective. There's more value in gathering in other people to support the effort and in being conscious of the emotional side of change.

When we talked with Lorraine, an administrator at a prominent New York law firm, she said, "I think that men are less adaptable to change, whereas women will accept it readily." She admitted that she was using her experience at a high-powered law firm to draw conclusions. After all, most of the senior attorneys were men, and as litigators, they were rewarded for being convinced that their side was always right.

Can Lorraine help her male colleagues learn how to adapt to a new structure?

Despite drawing from a limited sampling of men, Lorraine was correct. In our studies, we find that men are frequently less adaptable to change that is out of the ordinary. It's a price they pay for having a better focus and the ability to act fast.

Now, as her firm is in the midst of being taken over by a European firm, Lorraine finds she welcomes the change the new bosses are bringing in. Her male colleagues want to hold to the old structure. How can she help them adapt? One way is to use her natural tendency to research and reach out. She started e-mailing her counterparts in Europe to find out exactly how the management works in their organization. She now has lots of examples of how the merger partner has succeeded in bringing in new litigation business. And they need the help of Lorraine's firm to handle the extra workload.

See Chapter 15 for more about men and women handling change in the workplace.

External Changes

In a tragedy, the male approach is to grab the reins. Women will explore their options, negotiate, and try to avoid drastic consequences.

We will talk about several people whose lives are very different because of tragedies. Other, less dramatic external changes, such as a change in a commuting pattern, can also be a fork in the road. When a schedule change for Sheila's commuter bus made it difficult to get to her job on time, she started asking deeper questions. Was her unrewarding job really worth the aggravation when what she really wanted passionately was to write? Her teenage girls needed her to support them financially, but at forty, when was she going to try to achieve her own dream? After talking and complaining about it with her friends and children for several months and researching jobs in her local community, she decided to take the plunge. A man in the same position may have made the same decision, but if so, he would have done it with less talk.

While women are making their choices, the people around them are more likely to hear about the process. A man will complain less and then appear to act suddenly. Nicole, a successful consultant, observes, "It appears that women are overt about it—make an announcement that they're on a mission and typically want external affirmation that they're doing the 'right thing.' Men seem to decide to make the change in a more internalized way, and then one day, you just notice it." She goes on to say that "men compartmentalize events into 'mental boxes,' while women feel and live through changes longer and with more investment in its outcomes. I don't think men go through constant introspection and don't have to deal with multiple conflicting issues that change involves."

Chapter 16 provides more information about men and women managing the impact of external changes.

Finding What Works Best for You

All told, our research shows that men and women respond much differently to outside challenges such as change, with each gender following a course that was laid down by nature and by our own society. The point to remember is that there is no "best" way to react to change. The right way is the way that works for you, regardless of whether you are a man or a woman.

In conducting seminars on managing change over the last decade in many U.S. cities, we've learned a lot about the differences between men and women as they face change, both good and bad, both personal and professional. In this book, we share some of their stories with you to illustrate where knowing these differences has helped make change easier.

Differences between male and female styles also show up in other studies. For example, in the MBTI, a popular personality test, women are more likely to approach situations emotionally, while men take a more rational approach. Research on the male and female brain also shows distinct differences in emotionality, language capability, and spatial ability.

Men and women find peace of mind when they understand that if their partner has a different way of responding to change, it is not a sign of rejection. They learn to be more accepting of the different ways that men and women cope.

Women who understand these principles do not get offended when men choose to seek out an action plan rather than talk. Men sometimes act in an impulsive way; a woman can realize at these times that her man is living out his male destiny. When men and women achieve this deep understanding of how the other works best in crisis, they come to have a more satisfying and happier relationship throughout life.

Chapter 4

Discovering Your Gender Change Style

WHAT'S YOUR GENDER CHANGE STYLE? EACH OF US APPROACHES change in our own unique way. How likely are you to use a female strategy when approaching change? How much do you lean toward the male strategy? You can use the Change Style Worksheet at the end of this chapter to find out where you fit.

Our research shows that for both genders, there's a natural underlying rhythm to coping with change. Change is as constant as the seasons. Both men and women have a natural aptitude for managing change rhythms in very different ways. Learn how to identify the situations in which your natural style works best, the times when you can step forward and act with confidence. Understand the times when the opposite style is more useful to you and how you can borrow those actions.

You'll soon discover how change has three predictable steps, no matter whether it's a happy or unhappy change, a large change or a small one, a change you've requested or one that is visited upon you. We'll describe the characteristics of each of the change steps.

In this chapter, you'll learn the specific concrete ways that ordinary people use change rhythms to make change work in their lives. You'll also see how men and women approach each of the three change steps.

The feminine change style makes it easier to deal with the first one of the change steps, while the male change style works better during the second change step. Both genders have their unique advantages in the third and final change step. You will understand how to recognize each one. We'll explain how to deal with these change steps in the best way possible.

When Men Experience Change

Meet Tom Sullivan. When faced with change, he wants to act, not talk. When Tom responds to changes, he is likely to jump into action, but it's not always the best road to try. If the first action doesn't work out, he'll move on quickly to try out a new scheme.

When Tom is faced with change, he wants to act, not talk.

Take the time Tom and his wife, Sara, moved into a new house. Tom had been anxious to move. He'd overseen the building of the new house and was proud of it. There was much to do once the movers left.

Sara wanted to go room by room and get the furniture in place and then open the boxes and talk about what the room would look like.

Tom just had to get into action. He happened on the box of framed pictures first. He wouldn't stop until he hung every one. He put them where they'd been over the furniture in the old house. The arrangement wasn't that bad. It was just that they got into some rather odd places and it wasn't practical to move them without repainting.

If Tom had been more understanding of the ways women meet change, he would have given his wife time to visualize each room. Things might also have worked better if Sara had known that Tom, following the male rhythm of managing the change of a move, needed to accomplish something within the first five minutes of getting into the new house. She then could have visualized at least one room beforehand and sketched it out so Tom could get into immediate action.

When Women Experience Change

Eve Masters, a participant in our research, is another type of person. It takes her a while to come up with a suggestion for change, but when she does, it's likely to work out pretty well.

When faced with change, Eve will think it through, do her research, and talk with others about the best approach. Sometimes she takes so much time in doing this that the need

> Eve thinks change through, does her research, and talks with others.

or opportunity passes her by. But if it's still timely, her solution usually works out pretty well.

Eve wanted to get a group together to go out for a lunch to celebrate the retirement of a key member of their work group. The retirement would make a change in the way the team worked, so Eve felt it was important to mark the occasion.

First, she had a chat with the retiring team member and made sure a lunch with his workmates was something he would enjoy. They set a date.

She started a week ahead of time, first making sure the right people were asked. Then she went about researching the nearby restaurants. She called up the three likely choices, asking how long it would take them to serve a party of eight at lunch and what their usual tab was. Then she made the reservation. She circulated an e-mail to make sure everyone invited knew the time and the place.

Things worked out splendidly, and everyone felt the rituals of retirement had been properly observed.

She also applied the same thoughtful strategy to shopping for a mortgage. Rates had been very low, so she and her husband felt it was the right time to refinance. She called banks in the area and also searched the Internet for the best deal. She kept doing this for so long, hoping to get the optimum rate, that rates everywhere had gone up by the time she was done. Was it any wonder that her husband said "I told you so."

Differences Work

Both the female and male change styles can succeed, but some situations favor the male style and others the female style. When immediate action is required and there's an apparent right thing to do, it's better to approach change in the masculine style. Just do what's necessary. However, when the outcome is less apparent, and there is time to ponder, the feminine approach works better.

The more we understand the opposite style, the easier it is to handle change well. If someone who has a strong feminine change style faces a situation in which immediate action is required, she can rely on the opposite gender. Or she can try the masculine style of taking action. It's more stressful to act in another style, so we recommend doing it only when necessary.

Here's another example. Dick and Rosa are neighbors who live in a small town. Their state has approved the opening of a large casino in their county. This development will change the whole character of the town. Both Dick and Rosa have been active in the neighborhood association working to preserve the elements of town life that residents love. In Chapter 6 and again, in Chapter 16, we discuss the ways Dick and Rosa use their different approaches to change, one male and one female, to work through the three necessary change steps. Dick wanted to move right into action, but Rosa's desire to think things through slowed their team down to a workable plan, the result of combining their typical male and female approaches to change.

Each person must move through the three steps of change to cope with it successfully. Men and women cope in very different ways, but neither gender can ignore these three essential steps. The next three chapters show you how to recognize these three steps and how you can use your natural strengths to move through them.

What's Your Change Style?

Answer these questions about yourself. Which is your most natural, your first and easiest response? Check *yes, maybe,* or *no.*

		Yes	Maybe	No
1.	During change, I have to find out what others are doing.	❏	❏	❏
2.	When I realize things have changed, I take action immediately.	❏	❏	❏
3.	I hold back from giving my suggestions until I'm sure I'm right.	❏	❏	❏
4.	I like to give my opinions.	❏	❏	❏
5.	It's important for me to find out how others feel before I act.	❏	❏	❏
6.	I don't usually like to ask how to do something.	❏	❏	❏
7.	I'm more emotional when things are changing.	❏	❏	❏

	Yes	Maybe	No
8. Rules are made to be broken.	❏	❏	❏
9. Good solutions take time, especially during change.	❏	❏	❏
10. It's more important that people be useful than nice.	❏	❏	❏
11. Change in one part of my life affects all the other parts.	❏	❏	❏
12. I like to get goodbyes out of the way fast.	❏	❏	❏

How to calculate your gender change style:

To calculate your masculine change style score, look at the even-numbered questions. Subtract the number of "No" answers from the number of "Yes" answers.

For example, if you answered "Yes" to four even-numbered questions, and "No" to two even-numbered questions, your score would be two: four minus two. On the other hand, if you answered "yes" to only one even-numbered question and "no" to five of them, your score would be a negative four (one minus five).

Masculine score (M) = _____

In the same way, take the number of your "Yes" answers to odd-numbered questions, and subtract from it your number of "No" answers. This is your feminine change style score.

Feminine score (F) = _____

What your score means:

M score is 1 to 6. Your natural style during change uses most of the behaviors we call masculine.

M score is –6 to 0. You tend not to make much use of masculine ways to manage change.

F score is 1 to 6. Your natural style during change tends toward the approaches we call feminine.

F score is –6 to 0. You tend not to use feminine approaches to handling change.

Analyzing your score, for women:

If you're a woman, and you had a high feminine style score and low masculine style score, you're typical of most women in our studies.

If you had a high feminine style score and a high masculine style score, you make good use of your natural change style and have also learned to use the opposite gender's change style when needed.

If you had a low feminine style score and a low masculine style score, we suggest you start learning more ways to handle change, beginning with those most natural to women.

If you had a low feminine style score and a high masculine style score, you've adapted yourself to live and work in a masculine world. It should be easy for you to expand your change style to include the more feminine ways of coping with change.

Analyzing your score, for men:

If you're a man and you had a high masculine style score and a low feminine style score, you're typical of most men in our studies.

If you had a high masculine style score and a high feminine style score, you make good use of your natural change style and have also learned to use the opposite gender's change style when necessary.

If you had a low masculine style score and a low feminine style score, we suggest you start learning more ways to handle change, beginning with those most natural to men.

If you had a low masculine style score and a high feminine style score, you've learned how to handle change in a way that's more natural to women. It should be easy for you to expand your change style to include the more masculine ways of coping with change.

PART II

Change Steps and Change Skills

In the first three chapters of this section, we'll take you through the three steps that are essential for any change—*Say Goodbye, Move Through the Middles,* and *New Beginnings*—with a focus on how men and women approach each one differently. Chapter 8 introduces the five elements of the Brock Method to help you increase your capability to manage change.

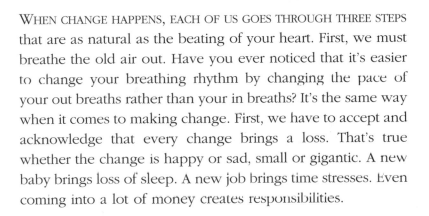

Chapter 5

Approaching Change Step 1: Say Goodbye

WHEN CHANGE HAPPENS, EACH OF US GOES THROUGH THREE STEPS that are as natural as the beating of your heart. First, we must breathe the old air out. Have you ever noticed that it's easier to change your breathing rhythm by changing the pace of your out breaths rather than your in breaths? It's the same way when it comes to making change. First, we have to accept and acknowledge that every change brings a loss. That's true whether the change is happy or sad, small or gigantic. A new baby brings loss of sleep. A new job brings time stresses. Even coming into a lot of money creates responsibilities.

Change Step 1: Say Goodbye

Remember the three change steps? Here's a reminder:

1. Say goodbye.
2. Move through the Middles.
3. Start a new beginning.

No matter whether you're a woman or man, you can learn to navigate every step of change more effectively. This chapter will cover the first essential step of change, *Say Goodbye*. In Chapter 6, you'll discover how to use your personal change style to navigate the important second step of change, as you move through the Middles. Chapter 7 will show you how to complete the change cycle with *New Beginnings*.

An Overlooked But Crucial Step

Say Goodbye is the most important and most commonly overlooked step of change. The feminine change style has an advantage in this first change step, but men have their unique strengths here too. Most women we talked with found it easier to spend the time thinking about what was going away in the change. They could understand that acknowledging the loss of the comfort of the old was the key to dealing with change. They could think about the positives of the old situation and be nostalgic for them.

Doris felt this way when she lost her beloved dog, Malcolm. She gave away all but a few of his things to a pet adoption center. She kept a few cherished items in the spot in the sun where he liked to sleep. Whenever she saw them she thought of Malcolm, remembering his antics with a smile. She also felt nostalgic for his love and companionship. By doing this, she was completing the first step of change. Someday she will get another dog, but she will wait until she feels she's ready to accept the new pet as an individual and not a copy of Malcolm.

You know you're in the first step of change when you notice the following:

- You can't believe what's just happened.
- You keep hearing that what's coming won't work.

- You're looking hard for someone to blame, even if it's yourself.
- Your level of trust is down.
- Your risk tolerance is out of whack: you feel like risking either nothing or everything.

Moving On

Marjorie and Sam are a couple who demonstrate the female and male preferences for dealing with this first change step. For many years they'd run a popular clothing store in a small city in Illinois. Marjorie did the buying, customer relations, and display. Sam was a whiz at the financial end.

When a business slowdown forced a bankruptcy, Sam saw a quick solution to the financial problem. He'd already demonstrated his organization skills to the company that handled the bankruptcy by managing closeout sales. So it made sense to ask for a position traveling around the country, representing the company and closing down the bankrupt stores they were purchasing. It was a typical male solution to change, focusing on the specific problem to continue the income flow.

Marjorie, on the other hand, felt some of the negatives of the first change step, *Say Goodbye*. She distrusted the company. She wanted to blame someone for the failure of their store, and they were the closest candidates. She sank into a depression, believing she'd never get to use her skills in retailing again or see her many friends in the community. She wanted to just abandon it all and go for a long sail around the Caribbean.

Sam was smart. He let her spend some time feeling nostalgic, and then he suggested that she stage a gala goodbye party. Sam was able to get Marjorie involved in putting together the goodbye party for the closing of their clothing store. It represented an action for Marjorie that she was good at. It got her through the rough patch in the loss of the store.

It wasn't until after the party that Sam started feeling depressed. Their home was for sale, and as soon as it was purchased, he just felt he couldn't cope. Knowing that it's harder for a man to express the emotion of a loss, Marjorie helped him pick out some favorite keepsakes from the house. She talked about how they would make a special place for them in their new condo. This ritual helped Sam say goodbye to what he was losing.

A Sudden Loss

In another example, Joe's childhood friend, Gayle, faced another sudden change: the death of her sister in an auto accident. She received a phone call telling her that her sister and brother-in-law had been driving their son to college in Albany. An unseen patch of ice was the culprit, leaving Gayle's sister dead at the scene and her husband hospitalized with serious injuries. At first, it was impossible for Gayle to believe her sister was dead. They'd talked every day of their lives, mostly arguing over some small thing.

Then the blame game set in. Gayle blamed her brother-in-law for driving, her nephew for choosing to go to a distant college, even her sister for allowing her husband to drive when she knew his vision wasn't perfect.

Joe decided it was time to use his expertise in helping others manage change. As a long-time friend, he jumped in to help with the funeral arrangements. This left Gayle free to talk with the many relatives and start her own grieving for her sister. She was also needed to help her brother-in-law and nephew.

Balancing and Expanding Your Natural Style As You Say Goodbye

When men and women meet change, an understanding of how the opposite gender handles it creates more productivity and happiness. If the situation requires immediate action, and there's an obvious right path, then the male approach works best. If there's more time and no clear solution, the female approach of networking and research is better.

However, there are other times when we have to borrow from the opposite style to make the change work. In this section, we explain how men and women react during the three steps of change and how those reactions illustrate each gender's particular skills. You can then try each one out, even if it's not your natural change style.

The most important tool for navigating the first steps of change is to accept the reality of emotional losses. What are you losing? What are other people losing? Think of all levels. What is the measurable external loss, and what is the internal loss?

Resistance to saying goodbye is also natural. It's not necessarily negative. Resistance is a force that tends to oppose or slow down motion. Just be sensitive to the difference between healthy resistance and resistance that impedes your daily functioning.

For example, when Sam and Marjorie were moving, Marjorie initially wanted to postpone the move for six months. She rationalized that she wanted time to see her garden bloom one more time. It didn't mean she wasn't willing to go; she just needed some time to adjust. Sam agreed to go along with the extra time. Actually, when he thought about it, he realized he'd need some time to sell the house. If business needs meant he had to fly out earlier, they agreed that would be all right, too.

Marjorie didn't say it directly to Sam, but she found out that after he did start spending time in the new location, he missed his old ties. They were able to talk about it, and Sam recognized that moving had an emotional component he hadn't considered.

For those who have been deeply affected, the first change step may take up to two years. It goes through stages, lessening in severity after two weeks, then again after two months, and after a year. You may feel the loss in terms of physical symptoms or a reduced capacity for work. Some of this is a natural reaction to change; however, if after two weeks you find you still cannot function, we advise you to think about seeking professional help.

Accept the reality of emotional losses.

The more female strategy of reaching out and talking to others about your feelings can help move you through the first change step and say goodbye in a timely fashion. You may also try expressing your feelings in an artistic way. Start keeping a diary, or take up painting. It doesn't matter if you aren't talented this way. It's the expression that's important. There was a time in our society when we could all express ourselves in artistic ways. Considering everything critically is a recent development.

Rituals of mourning are healing. When change happens, create a symbol or a ritual and give it a place in your mind or in your home for something that is lost. Doris was doing this when she made a special place in her home for her picture of her dog after he died. It reminded her of the playfulness of his personality and usually made her smile.

Mark the endings. Rituals of goodbye can help make a change like job displacement easier. Take a piece of the old way with you. When the Almaden winery was sold to developers, for instance, the management gave clippings from the rose garden to employees.

Knowing What to Keep with You

Kurt had been a pilot for Western Airlines for five years, but he lost his job when the company was sold to Delta and downsized. He went to the Employee Store at the Los Angeles Airport and bought a poster with Western's signature big red "W" logo on it. (Actually, he discovered that the store had nearly sold out of all items with the big red W logo in a few hours.) He found a place for the poster in his home. Kurt went on to find a successful and satisfying job as a corporate pilot for a large California software company, but he still notices the poster and remembers his time at Western Airlines.

Define what is over and what will continue.

Define what is over and what will continue. Be very specific. If you don't mark what is over, you along with others are likely to keep on doing things the way they have always been done.

Another example here is Vivien, who is newly widowed.

Vivien's friends are mostly couples, and that's the way she's been used to entertaining. In addition to giving herself space for grieving for her husband's death, she also sat down and made a list of how her life would change. One was that the way she entertained would be different. Though most of the couples she'd known when her husband was alive wanted to include her, it often became awkward to be the third wheel. Though she didn't try to keep forcing the issue, nor did she withdraw from life. When the time came to move into a more expanded social life, she had said goodbye to couples-only entertaining and reached out to other single people and to mixed groups of couples and singles, thus allowing her to include the friends from her marriage in her entertainment plans.

Acknowledge what you see with empathy, but stay clear on goals, maintain standards, and plan for strong reactions. First of all, be kind to yourself. When change happens, follow the advice of airline cabin crews: First, find your own oxygen mask, and then take care of the child beside you. If you fall apart with the change, you have no resources to share with others.

When the Huff family moved from urban Chicago to a suburb of Houston, their twin girls were in their junior year of high school. The girls were distraught about leaving their friends and favorite classes. At the new school, they fell behind in some of their classes and were apathetic about joining the local social activities. The parents wisely distinguished between acceptable and unacceptable behavior. "I understand how you feel, but I'm not going to let you drop out of school." Other strong reactions to change include anger and foot dragging.

In general, it's better to bring losses out into the open, acknowledge them, and express your concern for the people affected. Most of us are

Bring losses out into the open, and express your concern for the people affected.

uncomfortable when it comes to discussing our losses, feeling that it stirs up trouble. Discussing the loss is not what causes trouble; rather, problems stem from the pretense that loss doesn't exist. It helps everyone recover more quickly if things can be discussed.

If you find it easier to take the more female approach to change, you're going to have an advantage in going through the first change step—you're likely to feel all right about taking the time necessary to say goodbye to what's being lost. You'll find it easier to acknowledge the emotions you and those around you are going through. Even though it's difficult to talk about loss, you'll do it.

Work on building trust during times of change. It's natural during change to distrust all but those closest to us. The opposite approach usually works better during turbulent times. Not only should you trust more, you should also make it a point to show others that you trust them.

It helps build trust even by acknowledging that another person has influenced you. It can be something small. For example, you can say, "Helen, I wore this red scarf today because you said you liked it."

During change, it's important to focus on communicating, even though sometimes you don't feel like it. Also acknowledge the contribution others are making to you. Take

> Build trust by telling others how they've influenced you.

risks, but take the time to make them calculated. This usually means reaching out and doing some research and, if possible, testing the waters before you plunge. These moves toward building trust during change come more easily to women.

The first step of change is an important foundation for handling change. Many people like to jump right into the new, but they will always be haunted by the knowledge that they never came to terms with the past. Depending on the extent of the change, the first change step—*Say Goodbye*—can take a couple minutes or a couple months, but it's important to spend the time.

Chapter 6

Approaching Change Step 2: Move Through the Middles

SOONER OR LATER, CHANGE REQUIRES THAT WE MAKE A BRIDGE to the new situation. We try temporary ways of dealing with what's new. We put together something to be able to cope. We call this second change step *Move Through the Middles.* The male tendency toward action gives men an advantage in this step. But you can use it, whether you're a man or woman.

The best advice concerning this change step is to get through it as fast as possible and realize that you're in a vulnerable position. Put in what's necessary to get the essentials taken care of safely, even if it's temporary.

You know you're in the second step of change when you notice the following:

- Your productivity is way down.
- There's a lot of confusion about which way to go.
- You feel uncomfortable and out of control.
- The old way seems wrong, but you still feel nostalgia for it.

Sam and Marjorie made it through the Middles only when Sam was able to convince Marjorie that they could be partners in his new job organizing bankruptcy sales for clothing stores. After he reminded her that effective clothing sales depend on appealing displays and savvy customer relations, she was able to realize he needed her skills. Because of the appealing displays of merchandise and excellent customer service at the closedown sale, the project was a tremendous success.

Marjorie thought that probably she wouldn't go with Sam to every sale, but going to the first one helped her move on and think about what she wanted her new life to be. She'd moved through the difficult Middles without even thinking about it. She has now started on the third change step in a natural organic way.

Balancing and Expanding Your Natural Style in the Second Change Step

Move Through the Middles is the transition between the old and the new. Because it is a period of vulnerability and discomfort, getting through this period quickly is wise. So is focusing on what you can control. The control bull's-eye is a tool to help you figure out where you can feel control.

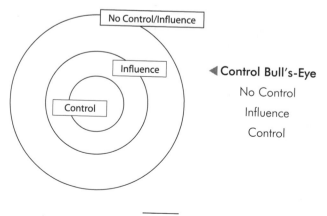

No Control/Influence

Influence

Control

◀ **Control Bull's-Eye**
No Control
Influence
Control

When you think about the particular change you're going through, what do you see that you can control? What's in the center of your bull's-eye? We can always control our own attitudes about any change. Usually, we can control the amount of information we get about it, along with the people and the times we choose to ask for support.

Let's take the example of Vivien, the recent widow we encountered in the last chapter. At the center of her bull's-eye was her own attitude about the death of her husband. So was her decision about whether she would move from her large and elegant home. She could reach out to others to find out how they handled similar situations and do research on the options available to her.

Then comes the middle circle, which includes the things you believe you can influence. These are events in which you have some input, but so does someone or something else. It could be how your family and friends think about the change or even whom you tell about it.

In the case of Vivien, she had influence over how she chose to mourn her husband and how long she would stay in a period of withdrawal from her life. Her children, other relatives, neighbors, and social customs had something to say, too. Once the time had come for resuming a social life, others had a say, but in the end, she had plenty of influence in whether she would continue to entertain in her home.

Focus on what you can control.

The outermost circle is the one representing all the effects of the change over which you have no influence or control.

For Vivien, this portion of the bull's-eye was filled with facts like her husband's death and the size of his estate. She chose to not blame herself or worry about these issues over which she had no control.

In the Middles step of change, try not to think about anything in the outer circle. Concentrate your time and energy on what you can control. Use the Control Bull's-Eye Worksheet at the end of this chapter to figure out what your three levels of issues are for the important changes you're facing.

Vivien used the Control Bull's-Eye Worksheet to concentrate her time on the center of the circle. She reached out to widows' support groups and found out what others had done in similar situations. She also learned a lot about ways other people had handled grief and realized she was going through it normally.

She focused time on whether she wanted to stay in her large house, again researching what the options were. It was in talking with her real estate agent that she found out that other single people in her age group had active social lives.

She talked with her children about the length of time she'd stay in formal mourning and let them know her feelings, but other than that she didn't think much about what other people thought. As it was, a fairly short period of about six months felt right.

In the outermost part of the bull's-eye, she was able to let go of most of her guilt about her husband's death and her concern that they hadn't planned their finances as well as they might have. Instead, she focused on how to use what she had.

Changing Other People's Minds

Take that bull's-eye again. For more important changes, you need to deal not only with the control center, you also have to move into the middle circle. You may have to change others' minds and behaviors and help them react more effectively and productively to change. The most powerful approach to changing someone's mind is to appeal to his or her values. Here is an example of how another study participant, Beth, did this with her mother.

Mrs. Hall, Beth's mother, had lived in West Virginia all her life. Beth wanted her to come to Chicago to attend her college graduation. She first appealed to her mother's appreciation for education and dislike of wasting money by sending her a non-refundable airline ticket to Chicago for the date of the graduation ceremony. This got Mrs. Hall beyond the immovable stage, but she was skeptical about even boarding a plane. Finally she succumbed to the natural pull of curiosity. As part of her carryon luggage, she brought a large bag of her homemade cinnamon rolls fresh from the oven. Their fragrance spread throughout the small plane, and she starting sharing them with other passengers and crew. It became a party, and Mrs. Hall got praise for something else she valued: her culinary skills. By the time the plane landed, she was ready to call her friends to recommend flying to all of them.

It was in this reasoned way that Beth changed her mother's mind. Being able to influence others is often important in getting through the second change step, the Middles.

We have found that men seem to know intuitively what can be controlled and what should just be ignored. In the Middles, they tend to create an example to follow. Women, on the other hand, are more likely to use talking to change minds.

Whether you're male or female, before you can change others' minds, you have to get them to move through four levels of openness to the change. They are likely to be some form of the following:

- Immovable
- Then critical
- Then curious
- And finally enthusiastic

No one moves from being immovable to being enthusiastic without going through the two stages in between.

Get through the transition fast. Like the molting stage of a bird or reptile, it's the period when you're at your most vulnerable. Skate fast. Expect a dip in productivity in the Middles. Why? Focus on priorities. It's like crossing the street in a crowded downtown. You know where you want to go. Don't hesitate, even though it may seem natural to do so for any of the following reasons:

- You're learning new things.
- You may not be clear about goals.
- You may want to rush forward, while others want to go back to the old ways.
- You—or most of us, anyway—feel tired and less than organized.

Check for unnecessary strains or changes. Review your rules to see if they are right for the new situation. This is a time for shedding old rules that no longer serve you.

Working with a Process

Dick and Rosa were the president and vice president of a neighborhood association confronted by the challenge of the casino coming to their community. They were bound by a rulebook that governed what neighborhood association officers could and could not do. It had been compiled by an overzealous and underchallenged board a decade earlier. For example, the president had no say in communication to the community; that was the realm of the vice president. This had stemmed from an earlier situation, in which the vice president was also the owner of the town paper and a jealous guardian of his power.

Dick just wanted to ignore the rules and move into action, but Rosa suggested that they set the process in motion to modify the rules. They were both right in that they needed to move ahead quickly and definitively and to do it in a way that also earned them long-term support from the group. This team approach worked effectively. Dick's action orientation got the high-priority items identified and acted on, and Rosa made sure the critical human issues were at the top of the list.

The lesson here is to make sure you set short-range goals and are careful not to over-promise. Communicate clear priorities, and take care of the "me" issue in a hurry. This is a time to go easy on yourself—don't start other less critical life changes that will scatter your energy. Nail down exactly what needs to be accomplished now, and let the other "necessities" be postponed.

> **Set short-range goals, and don't overpromise.**

Try Something New

It's natural to want to stick with the tried and true during times of change. Even though it feels a little awkward, it's a wonderful time to try out new ways to do things because old rules are breaking down. It's human nature to continue doing what we've always done. We shouldn't assume that because something was right yesterday, it's right today. Nor should we take it for granted that someone in the past has already tried out all the alternatives and found the best one.

Take small steps, and then be alert to the effect the change has on the situation. If you check in often, you have a chance to correct your course.

As an example, Dick and Rosa's community is also trying out a number of efforts to retain the feel of the town that residents love, despite the presence of the large casino. They are helping merchants connect with the casino's community vice president to familiarize him with what's available locally. But they also have been authorized to have a two-week campaign soliciting casino customers to come into the area with special sales. Every week they sit down to figure out which efforts are succeeding and which aren't.

The town council has used some of the lessons from the second change step, *Move Through the Middles*. It is focusing on what it controls or influences, creating several new ways to reduce strains, and trying tempo-**Take calculated risks.** rary measures to get the neighborhood through the difficulty. While these efforts are going on, the town and casino are poised to become, if not friends, at least reasonable partners in achieving their goals. This strategy was not one every town would take, and there were doubters along the way. Still, Dick and Rosa are proud of their efforts and the results. As Dick says, "It took courage, creativity, and teamwork to meet this change challenge."

During the Middles, you have to take risks in order to move quickly. The best strategy is to gather as much evidence as you can so you can make these calculated risks instead of blind stabs in the dark. This is where the female approach of reaching out for research combines well with the male tendency to fast action. When only one style is used, you will find that you tend to end up with either unnecessary mistakes or inaction.

Once you've cleared the Middles change step, then you're ready to move into the third and last step, starting your *New Beginnings*. That's the focus of Chapter 7.

Control Bull's-Eye Worksheet

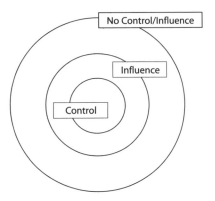

Change I'm facing: _____

Issues I control	Issues I influence	Issues I have no control over

Use this list to allocate your time in dealing with the change. Spend most of your effort on items in Column 1, the things you can control. Then spend some time on the items in Column 2, over which you have some influence. Try not to spend time or worry about the items in Column 3.

Chapter 7

Approaching Change Step 3: New Beginnings

THIS STEP, *NEW BEGINNINGS*, IS THE ADOPTION OF NEW BEHAVIORS that reflect the changed situation. Both women and men are good at this, but the two genders tend to express their new behaviors differently.

Women tend do more research and build up more slowly to a new start. Men just do it. They may sometimes forget to voice their *New Beginnings* intentions to others until later. Men are more proactive. Some men can be frustrated by what they see as a female tendency toward procrastination.

Often, the extra time that women spend in preparation for change allows them to come up with less traditional, more creative solutions. We'll describe how the feminine and masculine approaches to change are different in this stage and where each gender has its own advantage.

You know you're in the third step of change when you notice the following:

- People start catching you in new behaviors.
- Your instinct is usually to do it the new way.
- Trust and a feeling of optimism are building.

This is the light at the end of the tunnel. It may take a while for the differences to become apparent. Usually what happens first is you start talking about what things will be like when the change is in place. Then you start to notice that every now and then you are thinking and behaving in a different way. Finally, the new becomes habit.

In the story of Sam and Marjorie, the couple we met in Chapter 5, when they were facing a major move, Marjorie made it through the third change step, *New Beginnings,* by working with her friends and customers. She was able to find a way to make them a permanent part of her new life as well as a way to incorporate her old customers in the new business. She had kept detailed records of their sizes and style preferences. She used it to set up a mail order business, offering them choice items from the stores that she and Sam closed down. With a new digital camera, she took pictures of her recommendations and e-mailed them to the appropriate customers.

We also remember Gayle from Chapter 5, where she faced the sudden death of her sister. As Gayle entered the third change step, she started forming a closer relationship with her nephew. He now stays with Gayle and her husband when he's on break from college. He has his own room at their home, and she takes great pains to always have the foods he likes in the refrigerator. Despite enjoying her closer relationship with her nephew, Gayle has realized that she and her husband have lost a lot of privacy in this change.

At first she felt threatened that her nephew was going to make too many demands on her time. She's an artist, and she feared the new responsibility might take away from her creativity. However, she was able to organize a more defined studio space in the house, and she actually finds that she's working better now than she had when she was spread out over the whole house. She does ask that her nephew (and her husband) respect her privacy when she's in the studio.

Balancing and Expanding Your Natural Style in the Third Change Step

New Beginnings is literally the beginning of the new, and it happens only after you've spent time in the first two change steps, *Say Goodbye* and *Move Through the Middles*. The first thing to do is paint a clear picture. What do you want to have happen? The more specific and concrete you can be, the more likely things are to happen that way.

If it's a new residence that's in your future, actually draw a picture. The quality of the art doesn't matter. Stick figures are fine. You might

| Paint a clear, specific picture of the future.

choose to do it with words. What are the details? What will it look like, feel like, sound like, even smell like to be there? Who will be with you?

Here's the picture that Sandy made of the retirement home she was creating for herself. "It will be in a cold climate and will have a small patio where I can enjoy cool summer evenings. I'll have a place for my mother's large Oriental carpet. There will be a small kitchen and dining area where I'll entertain old and new friends. The living room will be filled with books, music, and flowers and have lots of comfortable chairs." She kept this image in front of her for a year, modifying it as she thought of things important to her. She now lives in her ideal home in Portland, Maine, and enjoys her volunteer work with the museum and her new life.

We'll learn more about creating a personal vision in the next chapter. It's one of the five critical change skills in the Brock Method.

Men and women are both skilled at creating a vision for the future. The skills just come out a little differently. Men's visions are centered on action. For example, Larry—whom we'll meet in the next chapter—saw himself after a major weight loss "walking the full eighteen holes without panting." Women, on the other hand, emphasize overcoming vulnerabilities and connecting to other people.

Explain the reasoning behind the new beginning.

After losing a lot of weight, Marisa (whom you'll also meet soon) kept a picture of herself at the new weight on her desk to reinforce how good she looked.

Explain the purpose behind the outcome. In the last step of change, it's our nature not to want to talk about the new beginning until it is firmly in place. This is true especially for men. The irony here is that it's the communicating that hammers in the solid foundation and builds the support walls.

Set out the steps for yourself and anyone else involved in creating the new reality. What will you do today? Tomorrow? By the end of the year? Every year, smart business owners write a plan for the year ahead. This should be a part of our New Year's routine for our personal lives. We first sum up what we've accomplished and feel good about that and celebrate it. How have our dreams changed? Then we forecast what will change and what the specific plan is for next year. A lot will come up we don't anticipate, but we know what we want the theme of the next year to be. None of this has to be elaborate. But thinking it out, talking about it, and writing it down helps to make it happen.

Be consistent. Avoid common traps, such as advocating new ways while rewarding people for following the old ones. Another trap is to preach risk taking but reward a lack of mistakes. The new beginning takes hold when someone starts to use the new behaviors and becomes successful. The change will happen when you

| Practice what you preach.

start trying to do things a different way. First, you'll do it sporadically. Then as success builds, it becomes a habit.

If you're working with other people to make change work, like Dick and Rosa in their town council, you'll find that first it's only talk, but then a few incidences of the new behavior occur that you can celebrate. Finally, the new behaviors become a norm for the group.

When Rosa first put up the town Web site and online chat room, usage was low. But she got an artist council member to make some drawings of what he cherished in the town. She got a few people to express their feelings, successes, and disappointments. She publicized them on the site with their photographs. Soon others joined in, especially as they got responses and realized that many others felt as they do. *New Beginnings* are likely to start with a few people showing how to do it; soon enough, others will get on the bandwagon.

Practically speaking, this means forgiving mistakes and encouraging questioning. In the initial phases of the new beginning, there will be mistakes. Most of us have to go through a trial-and-error phase of doing things a different way. Go easy on yourself. Try to practice new behaviors in low-risk environments. Ask for support from family and friends as you make your progress.

Break new behaviors down into manageable chunks. If the new changes are large and far-reaching, they may take a long time to be realized. Critics will have a field day. Quick successes reassure the believers, convince the doubters, and confound the critics.

This is what Marisa did when she set about to lose a substantial amount of weight. She set rewards for herself for each ten pounds lost (nonfood rewards, of course). Once it was a special set of bubble bath and candles. Then it was a group of potted herbs for her kitchen. When she achieved her end goal, it was clothes in the new size. And she hasn't forgotten to reward herself every month that she stays at her desired weight. Her treat could be as simple as a movie or a new book, or as public as celebrating with the people who supported her efforts to lose weight.

Reward risk taking, and recognize small successes.

In the next chapter, we'll take up the Brock Method, the five skills that you can cultivate to help you manage each of the three critical change steps more effectively and happily. You'll learn how men do it and how women do it and what we can learn from each other.

Chapter 8

Sharpening Change Skills for Men and Women: The Brock Method

THIS CHAPTER SHOWS YOU THE BROCK METHOD FOR MANAGING change better. It is a method developed from a model of change based on five years of research, teaching, and consulting. It illustrates the five skills proven to make change work. It shows how to become a master of each one. You'll be able to see where your change strengths and weaknesses are by using our specially designed Change Capability Worksheet at the end of this chapter.

In this chapter we will tell you the stories of real people who use change to help them lead happier, more productive lives.

Learning from Each Other's Strengths

The initial research for this chapter comes from Peace Corps research on what makes for a successful volunteer and what differentiates the people who opt out of the program and choose to come home early. Going through change is very often like moving into a new culture; the unstated rules are different. It's hard to figure out at first, but you can learn to do it. We believe that you can do it best using the five change skills.

Men and women have varying natural abilities on each of the five change skills. By understanding each other and learning from each other's strengths, we can be more effective and happier.

The Five Change Skills in the Brock Method

1. Personal Vision

2. Reframing

3. Emotional Resilience

4. Flexibility

5. Self-Sense

We believe that both men and women are happier when they live in an environment that supports them and that is consistent with their desires and strengths. What we do in this chapter is show you how to improve your five change skills so that you can create an environment that better supports your needs and strengths. We'll show you how to develop a personal vision, reframe, build emotional resilience, become more flexible, and increase your sense of self. These are the tools that men and women can both use to make change work better in their lives. The female tools and the male tools have some similarities, but they do differ from each other.

Of the five tools, men have a natural talent for creating a personal vision. They also tend to have a stronger sense of self. Women can do both of these as well, but they approach these skills from a more complex set of strengths and passions and a less traditional sense of self. Women have the advantage in reframing, emotional resilience, and flexibility. However, all can improve their ability in each of the five change skills. We'll tell you how with the Brock Method.

Using All the Tools You Need

In order for Stan or Mary to deal with change effectively, both must use the change tool kit. Mary had just retired from more than twenty-five years at a large national company. She liked the job there very much, and although she had several different assignments as a manager throughout her company career, she had never really done anything else. After the retirement party, Mary found herself crying at her desk. It wasn't that she was so unhappy to leave her job, but a feeling of emptiness overwhelmed her now that she was looking directly at retirement.

Mary needed to develop her five change skills to come out alive and well on the other side.

Stan, on the other hand, had a completely different reaction to his retirement. He had been a New York City fireman for thirty years. Now as a captain, he was in charge of the entire fire company in his district. His seniority allowed him to work in a fire district near his home.

His job was dangerous.

Over the years he had been injured many times, twice falling through burning roofs and lately into the basement of a building on fire. He had saved people's lives. He had carried them out of buildings. He was in charge of many younger men, but he was always with them when it came time to go to danger.

After thirty years, Stan was both physically and mentally tired. He was ready to leave the job. But a strange thing happened within a week of his retirement party. Stan found himself depressed. He felt totally old and useless. When he heard the sound of sirens, he always went to the window and looked out.

Stan needed to develop the five change skills to help him cope with this great change in the fabric of his life.

Change Skill 1: Create a Personal Vision That Stirs Your Passion

Personal Vision is the first element of the Brock Method. Without a sense of where you're going, change is unlikely to make sense. Research shows that in extreme situations, a clear vision of what you want out of life can be the difference between life and death. Those people in concentration camps who were determined to live to see their grandchildren had a better survival rate than those who had no life plan. Only doing what you're passionate about can add richness to life that will carry you through a period of rapid change.

> Only passions, great passions, can elevate us to great things.

What are your strengths and weaknesses? They are the foundation to creating your personal vision. One of the fundamentals in creating a vision for yourself is to know your strengths and weaknesses. Make sure your personal vision builds on your strengths and goes away from your weaknesses. Be confident and secure in your own strengths. Seize every opportunity to use them. Moving forward in strength is the key to success.

As for those struggling with weaknesses, which we all have, seek out others to help you in those areas. Be very open to accepting help from others in situations in which you don't feel strong. With this stance, change can be an engine of growth and an opportunity to have your vision come true.

Concentrate on your strengths. Research shows that most people spend 70 percent of their time focused on their problems (or in the Problems box, as we say). We grow up emphasizing and overcoming our weaknesses. But we must also make time to use our strengths.

Otherwise, you end up with the proverbial school for animals. "Once upon a time the animals got together and decided to found a school. There would be a core curriculum of six subjects: swimming, crawling, running, jumping, climbing, and flying. At first the duck was the best swimmer, but it wore out the webs of its feet in running class. And at first the dog was the best runner, but it crash-landed twice in flying class and injured a leg. The rabbit started out the best jumper, but it fell in climbing class and hurt its back. At the end of the school year, the class valedictorian was an eel, who could do a little bit of everything, but nothing very well."

Let's hear about Marisa and her winning battle to lose weight by using the personal vision tool. She sat down and figured out she was good at sticking to a reduced calorie diet during weekdays, but on the weekends she liked to enjoy mealtimes with family and friends. Rather than trying to go against this tendency, she devised a scheme where she banked some calories from very lean meals during the week. She was able, in moderation, to eat more lavishly over the weekend.

And Larry used the same tool with a similar issue, but as a man he used it somewhat differently. He was never going to give up his snacks while watching football games, but he loved going to the gym. He lost a significant amount of weight by doubling the amount of time he spent on the treadmill.

Now it's time to start creating your own personal vision. You can use the Mix 'n' Match Tool at the end of this chapter to start. Or just draw two lines down a blank sheet of paper to make three columns.

In the left-hand column, write down your strengths—everything you're good at. In the middle—the passion column—list the activities that stir your passions. Fill the last, or needs, column with needs that exist in your community that might be related to the first two columns.

Now comes the time to pick out some menus that you love. Pick one item from the strengths column, one from the passion column, and one from the needs column. First, see what might logically go together. Then stretch your imagination by picking randomly. One example that worked out to a rewarding vision was created by Penny. She combined her ability to speak French with her love for tennis and the need of the teens in her community to have rewarding summer activities. At first sight, there seemed to be no match. However, as she thought about it and talked with others, she formulated a plan to take teenagers interested in tennis to tennis camp in France. To her great delight, she has been able to make her vision a reality.

Start creating your own personal vision.

Henry, a middle-aged man caught in a dead-end job in a bland suburb, combined his ability in taxes and accounting and his passion for winter sports into a position as chief financial officer at a Colorado ski resort. He and his family love their new outdoorsy life.

At first, you may not come up with a personal vision that's right for you. Most of us need to let the ideas simmer for a while.

If your personal vision hasn't gelled, write down a couple of ideas and put them in a place you see every day. Talk to others about it. Think about it while you're doing other things. The "a-ha" should come in a week to ten days.

Make your personal vision of the future pass the 3-M test: Make it memorable, motivating, and meaningful. Engage the mind and heart, where possible.

Memorable

You won't do what you can't remember. An example of this is the original vision statement that NASA adopted in the 1960s. It read as follows: "The objective is to execute a launch vehicle into a nonorbit trajectory directed toward interstellar flight with the intent of descension on the nearest orbiting body and reverse ascension and re-entry inside of seven budgetary cycles." One of President Kennedy's speechwriters heard this and said, "What you mean is we're going to get a man on the moon by the end of the decade." Money and energy started flowing, and Neil Armstrong and Buzz Aldrin walked on the moon on July 20, 1969.

Motivating

An effective statement of the future has to be something that stirs your heart. It has to help you out of bed on rainy mornings and through the difficult times. The U.S. Post Office had a straightforward vision statement in the 1980s. It was "Our purpose is that every employee accomplish duties in the required manner." It was easy to remember, but hardly motivating. It contains none of the drama and romance of the words etched over the doors of many older post offices: "Neither snow nor rain nor heat nor gloom of night stays these couriers from the swift completion of their appointed rounds."

Meaningful

Your vision of the future is something that should really make a difference in everyday actions. Fred Smith, the charismatic CEO of Federal Express, had a vision of his courier service being different in that it got the package there next day *no matter what.* This came in handy when the manager of the small FedEx office in Nome, Alaska, was faced with a blizzard that closed the roads down one day. The following day, the sun shone, but the roads were still impassable. What did he do? He hired a helicopter for $10,000, way over his budget, and got all his packages delivered. In another organization, he would have been penalized. But what he did was consistent with Smith's vision, and he was rewarded. He was flown down to corporate headquarters in Memphis and the press was called in to the party. FedEx ended up getting a million dollars' worth of publicity.

Creating a Personal Vision: Two Examples

How often should your personal vision change? A major change in your environment is often a signal that it's time to revisit your personal vision. Do it at least yearly. Sit down and review what's happened to push you closer and what's hindering it. Then make a choice whether you want to revise your personal vision or not.

Mary did just that. She came to us asking if we could help her take control of the new life she was entering. We asked her to use the Mix 'n' Match Tool to create her personal vision of where she wanted her life to go.

At first Mary could only think of a couple of strengths. She knew she was good at managing other people and that she enjoyed it. She had also specialized in laboratory analysis and had used those techniques throughout her career. We encouraged her to look at other areas and at the nontraditional ways she excelled. This is easier for women to do than men. In our society, they've often had to do several things at once.

As she thought about it, Mary talked about how much her children loved her chocolate chip cookies and peanut butter fudge. She always got compliments on the desserts she served at parties. Her dried apricot pie was also a top seller at her church's fundraiser. What's more, she'd found a way to adapt recipes so they were healthier.

The passions column was easier for Mary. She'd always had lots of interests. Two of the entries were baking and working in her church. The last column of what was needed centered on her church's need for funds. She also felt some sense of devotion to getting the people around her to eat more healthful foods without having to sacrifice their dining pleasure to do it.

Because Stan was a friend, Mary tried to get him in to go through the same process with her. He was reluctant at first, but finally after seeing Mary's delight in her new life, he came by.

Stan's case was harder to work with. At first he wanted a quick solution. When he brought his Mix 'n' Match Tool back to us, it had one strength (fighting fires), one passion (seeing fires prevented), and one community need (you guessed it—the need to prevent fires).

It wasn't too much to work with, but in our conversations, he did mention he had participated in a program in which he went around to local businesses and helped them assess their fire prevention readiness. He ended up developing a volunteer fire prevention assessment program—a checklist of action items that businesses could use to prevent fires. He scheduled appointments and went to the site in his fireman's uniform.

This was a good solution for Stan because it didn't require much additional research. He was also able to put it into place without changing what he knew.

Change Skill 2: Reframing

Taking a new perspective on obstacles in your life can open up room for creativity and opportunity. We travel a lot and always used to dread a delayed flight. Several years ago, we started reframing the delay time as a chance to catch up on reading and talk to people we don't ordinarily get the chance to see and meet. It's useful to have a reframing "buddy."

As children, we had the capability to look at the world without blinders. This skill simply means "take a good look around you." When change happens, we tend to close ourselves into our group and draw the boundary lines tighter. Research on decades of U.S. Peace Corps volunteers has shown that the opposite is more effective. Use "the naive eye" to find new opportunities in your environment for managing change. This means looking at yourself and your life as if you were seeing it for the first time. Small children are very adept at this.

Women also have a natural ability when it comes to reframing because they are naturally more sensitive to their environments.

Peggy, one of the people we interviewed in our research, always needed ten minutes to explain to anyone who asked what she did for a living. She is a research technologist and is involved in some very exciting biomedical research. However, it wasn't very easy to explain, and she found most people tuned out after a minute. When her daughter went to kindergarten, she kept asking her mom what she did for a living. Knowing her daughter would remember only the basics, she said, "I help make medicines that make people feel better." Now, Peggy uses that explanation herself. The next time you're in a complicated change, try thinking how you would explain it to a six-year-old.

During periods of change, it's particularly important to notice the result that your actions have on others. Take an extra second after you've spoken or acted to see what the reaction has been. You may need to repeat, clarify assumptions, or change course.

Lisa learned this. When her company was merged into a larger one, she moved from California to New York. She needed to make only one blunder to realize she had to curb her sunny California optimism. New Yorkers were starting to discount her opinions as not thought through. It only takes an extra second to watch others' reactions to what you've done or said. Then you have a chance to course correct or continue as you were.

Develop your listening skills. This is something that women come by more naturally, but everyone can improve in this area by being aware of how we listen. In school, we're trained in reading, writing, and arithmetic, but almost never in listening. Make it a point to sum up what the other person is saying to you, especially for an important conversation. You can do it mentally. The average person thinks at 500 words per minute, but the fastest talker can only speak at 250 words per minute, so you have plenty of "mind space" to do a mental summary. It's a waste of a good conversation to spend the extra time just in thinking about what you're going to say next, the way most of us do.

Build your listening skills.

Change Skill 3: Develop Your Emotional Resilience

Stress and change are not always negative. At the right levels, they stimulate and lead to growth. It's reaction to stress that's so debilitating. No change is necessarily negative or positive; it's our reaction to it that makes it so.

Just acting calm and positive when stressed makes our brains take it better. In our research, we've noticed that those people who have emotional resilience find it easier to take change as a positive. The successful women we've talked with score highly on emotional resilience. How have they developed it?

One tool is to balance work, fun, family, social, spiritual, communal, and the other important elements of your life. Consider the various elements of your life. For most people, the important parts are the following:

- Work
- Relationship with husband or wife
- Relationship with children and parents
- Relationship with rest of family
- Relationship with friends
- Hobbies
- Other leisure activities
- Religious and community activities
- Time spent alone
- Time spent on personal growth

How much of your waking time do you spend in each of the above ten categories in an average month? The way you interpret these categories is up to you. You may want to add to or change the wording to describe your life better.

How I Spend My Time in an Average Month	
Work	_____%
Relationship with spouse	_____%
Relationship with children and parents	_____%
Relationship with rest of family	_____%
Relationship with friends	_____%
Hobbies	_____%
Other leisure activities	_____%
Religious and community activities	_____%
Time spent alone	_____%
Time spent on personal growth	_____%
TOTAL WAKING TIME IN A MONTH	100%

No one is likely to spend exactly 10 percent in each one, and the percentages do change in different stages of a life. However, we do recommend that you spend at least a little time in each category.

Having a life that's in balance gives space for recovery. That way when the time you spend in one category falls dramatically, as with a job layoff or a child who's leaving home, you've had practice in doing something else. A number of our clients have built up a successful second career from what was once a hobby.

Men tend to concentrate in a couple of categories to the exclusion of others because of their ingrained tendency to focus. On the other hand, it's quite natural for women to reach out to balance the elements of their lives. This could be because they've historically had to fulfill more roles than men do.

Sports coaches recommend that we train for stress, physically and mentally. The physical side is what you already know about good diet and sufficient exercise. Another part of resilience is to eat right, exercise, sleep enough, and minimize your bad habits.

Looking for another good way to cope with stress? Laugh more! Research on children shows they laugh 400 times a day. Experts recommend that adults laugh at least fifty times a day. How much is it for the average adult? In stress-laden India, Laughter Clubs are springing up all over because they've been found to reduce stress and illness.

Balance work, fun, family, friends, and the other important elements of your life.

Here's some ideas for creating a laughter routine in your life that you can practice daily:

- Make a video of one television show or movie that truly makes you laugh. Watch it at least once a week. The cable networks Comedy Central and Nick at Night are good resources.
- Keep a joke book or file, cutting out cartoons or stories that make you smile.
- Subscribe to any of the humor networks available online.
- Enlist a friend as a humor buddy and be responsible for creating a laugh for each other daily.
- Build a laugh into your daily fitness routine. It's great to practice when you're in the gym in front of a mirror. Exercise doesn't have to be grim.
- Form a Laughter Club in your community. You can find details at the club Web site, *www.worldlaughtertour.com*.
- Take a clowning class.
- Cultivate people and activities that make you laugh.

Plan recovery time. Sports champions and their coaches have learned that recovery is not so much about the length of time you allow yourself for recovery as it is about doing it at the right time. A ten-minute break can be very effective after a stressful situation. Winston Churchill observed that you can't just turn off your mind from worrying. You must shift to another activity, and that is why he took up painting.

| Plan recovery time.

The Huff family used this strategy during their move from Chicago to Houston. First, they each decided to increase the percentage of time spent with family for the first three months in their new home. They set aside a period that would be family time, when they'd share stories of adjusting to the new community. Each person promised to bring in at least one laugh. On one family Sunday, Ginger was having such a difficult time in her new school, she resorted to wearing a fake nose to get her laugh, but as time passed, she had some genuinely positive moments to share.

Change Skill 4: Increase Your Flexibility

As mentioned before, when change happens, you have three primary choices: do nothing, do more of the same with increased effort, or do something different. Charles Darwin observed that the species that are flexible in face of change have the best chance for survival.

Flexibility is easier for women, but we will give you specific tools to help everyone build flexibility. The historical roles women played as gatherers have developed the innate talent of being on the lookout for new ways.

Exercise your flexibility muscle. Love to learn and look out for new approaches and new skills to learn. Practice can increase your flexibility. And doing it in small ways compounds to more capability for large changes. If you're a golfer, try a new course every month or so. If you're a cook, try a new recipe every week. If you're a commuter, try new ways of getting there. These strategies can help if the old way is blocked or if you just need to reframe.

Men are target-focused; that is to say, they've been directed by society and genes to concentrate on one goal. Over the generations, they have been rewarded in exact proportion to how well they attain their defined goal. Attaining the goal generally meant narrowing the focus to one objective and putting the premium on constantly advancing toward that objective until it was reached. Over the years, men largely ignored issues like flexibility because this was a skill that was perceived to be weakening the march toward the target.

Exercise your flexibility muscle.

Focus on Small Goals

The "small wins" technique is an effective way of building your own flexibility. Big goals seem overwhelming. Often, people are discouraged before they even begin. The smart thing to do in life is to dream big. But in dreaming big we are sometimes intimidated by the size of our goals. The best way to handle this is by concentrating on small, immediate goals that lead to the measurable success of the larger goal.

It's just like a football game. The offensive team's overall goal is to make a touchdown, but frequently that goal can be almost a hundred yards away. Of course, the quarterback would love to cover those yards all at once with a Hail Mary pass. He'll gladly accept the touchdown that way. But experienced quarterbacks know that the most reliable way to score a touchdown is to complete a successful series of first downs. It may not be as exciting as a big pass, but concentrating on those small objectives is generally a better way to get the job done.

Imagine George, who wanted to lose 100 pounds. Why bother to even start? But when he started to think of it as losing ten pounds and then rewarding himself (preferably not with a food treat), then it became easier to act. He was able to improve his flexibility quotient by using the tools from this book. He decided he was going to enjoy his weekly golf by getting his buddies to try out four courses they didn't usually frequent. Everybody had a little more fun, and George got a bit more exercise, which helped with his weight loss program. He also decided he'd learn a new skill by taking a nutrition course at his local community college.

Change Skill 5: Increase Your Self-Sense

Why in the world are men able to walk into a new situation and appear to be supremely confident? A man's natural approach to increasing his sense of self includes complimenting himself on his good qualities and accomplishments. It takes a strong sense of yourself not to be buffeted about by winds of change. Take every chance you get to "know yourself."

Many of us, particularly women, have a hard time hearing a compliment and letting it register. It's easy to brush off congratulations on an achievement. Even when complimented

> Compliment yourself on your good qualities and accomplishments.

on a new dress, the answer is, "Oh, this old thing, I bought it on sale." At the same time, that same woman is likely to magnify any criticism. Fifty people can compliment her, but if one is critical, that's what she'll remember.

We have two suggestions for this. First, repeat every compliment to yourself several times until it registers internally. Second, listen carefully to criticism, but make a considered decision on whether to accept it, depending on whether it's accurate and well motivated.

There's magic in assuming the physical characteristics of confidence and showing that you can do it. What differentiates champion tennis players from middle ranks with the same ability? It's the way they behave between points. You don't find Andre Agassi or Pete Sampras slumped over after a bad play. They are confident and thinking about the next play rather than worrying about the last one. Researchers call this "the matador's walk." Act as if you'll have a positive outcome, and you're more likely to have it. Our human physiology makes a positive outcome more likely when we make that appearance. It's hard to get angry when you have a smile on your face.

> **Act as if you'll have a positive outcome, and you're more likely to have it.**

Becoming More Assertive

Assertiveness is a skill that most women need to learn. Meredith, a young woman working in the investment banking business, used assertiveness techniques for getting a promotion and salary increase. First, she defined exactly what she wanted. Then she put together the facts: what salary ranges were for her position, and what specifically she'd done for the organization. She determined who decided on her promotion and increase and how she could appeal to his or her motivations. She realized her supervisor felt overworked.

Meredith then volunteered to take over some of those duties and demonstrated she could handle them. As a result, she got a 20-percent raise at a time when few others were even getting raises in the single digits. A year later, she was promoted to the next level.

Form a Dream Team. We've established several as a way to help people handle life changes. The idea is to gather a group of five to twelve people who commit to meet regularly for a year. ▌ **Join a Dream Team.** Each person agrees to define a dream and then report progress on it at each meeting. Others listen and add suggestions and encouragement. There's magic in announcing your intent to others. And the energy that can come from a group of supporters goes a long way in helping your sense of self.

Making It Work

Mary and Stan have learned to improve all of their change skills.

For Mary, emotional resilience came fairly easily, and she added some flexibility routines into her life. After a couple of weeks of doing research in bookstores and on the Internet as well as talking with friends and fellow church members, she decided she would concentrate creating a "Get Your Just Desserts" table at the next church bazaar. It had fifteen of Mary's most popular healthful desserts for sale, and each one included the recipe, so buyers could re-create the dish at home. It took a lot of preparation and organization, but Mary was actually using her managerial skills as she staffed the table.

It was her sense of self that Mary wanted to work on. Even as a manager, she had doubts about herself, even though everyone else seemed to think she was pretty good. As the Just Desserts concepts grew, she worked with us to develop more assertiveness. She also took courses on how to publish a book and how to work in front of a television camera.

Now, several years later, Mary has published a cookbook and has appeared on several televised cooking shows. Her own *Get Your Just Desserts* show may be in the works.

This was a good solution for Mary because it capitalized on her personal strengths and passions, and it used her natural skill as a woman to reach out, research, and network when change happens. She used her natural emotional resilience and flexibility, and she reframed by taking her new life in small steps and modifying at each one.

In the next chapter, we'll show you how you can use the five change skills in navigating the major life changes that occur in marriage and divorce. Below, we have a worksheet to help you to evaluate your own capability for change. It's followed by an important tool that we'll refer to often, the Mix 'n' Match Tool, which you can use to unlock your creativity and discover the connections between your abilities, desires, and your community's needs.

Change Capability Worksheet

		Yes	No
1.	Do you periodically consider your life goals to see how you're doing?		
2.	Are you emotionally resilient?		
3.	Do you naturally meet stress with a positive attitude?		
4.	Do you have good posture?		
5.	Do you sleep at least seven to eight hours a night?		
6.	Do you watch what you eat and drink?		
7.	Do you exercise at least three times a week?		
8.	Is your time no more than 80 percent concentrated in one activity like work?		

	Yes	No
9. Are you able to laugh often?		
10. Do you have activities you use to renew yourself?		
11. Do you make it a point to try something new periodically?		
12. Do you break down big goals and problems into smaller pieces?		
13. Are you able to look at situations, problems, and activities from several different angles?		
14. Do you reward "small wins"?		
15. Do you have at least one reframing buddy?		
16. Are your listening skills excellent?		
17. Are you confident that you know yourself?		
18. Are you assertive when necessary?		

Calculate your score by counting up your "yes" answers and subtracting the "no" answers. The closer you are to a total of 18, the better your ability to manage change.

 0–5: Change challenged
 6–10: Have the basics of handling change, but capable of improvement
11–15: Capable and confident in times of change
16–18: A change master

Mix 'n' Match Tool for Creating Your Personal Vision

Resources	Passions	Needs
WHAT ARE YOU GOOD AT?	WHAT DO YOU LOVE TO DO? WHAT ARE YOUR PASSIONS?	WHAT NEEDS TO BE DONE IN YOUR COMMUNITY (OR THE ONE WHERE YOU WANT TO LIVE)? WHAT WILL PEOPLE PAY FOR?
R1.	P1.	N1.
R2.	P2.	N2.
R3.	P3.	N3.
R4.	P4.	N4.
R5.	P5.	N5.
R6.	P6.	N6.
R7.	P7.	N7.
R8.	P8.	N8.
R9.	P9.	N9.
R10.	P10.	N10.
R11.	P11.	N11.
R12.	P12.	N12.
R13.	P13.	N13.

Pick out appealing matches taking one item from each column. For example, you might combine R1, P7, and N3. Work fast, and don't screen any combination out at first.

Which combinations could represent your future? Pick a time in the future and ask yourself: What would perfection look like?

_____

_____

_____

_____

_____

_____

_____

_____

_____

_____

Sketch something here that represents your initial vision elements.

Realistic First Steps. How (and with whom) will you start working toward this personal vision? Think creatively, and list some possible first steps moving toward your vision.

Directions for Using the Mix 'n' Match Tool to Create Your Personal Vision

In the first column, start listing the resources you have. Your strengths are the beginning of the list. That's anything people tell you you're good at, from baking a perfect apple pie to having a great radio voice. Most people can come up with at least ten by not listening to that little voice many of us have, the one that says, "You shouldn't brag." In addition to strengths, you also have resources. Some people might have a big house, others a little extra time, and others a terrific support network, so fearing failure is not an issue.

In the second column, write down anything that stirs your passion. It could be anything from a beautiful rose to holding a baby. A sport may be a passion, like golf, or maybe you love foreign travel. Try to list at least ten; more is even better. Some of your passions may be the same as your strengths, but this is not necessarily the case. You may have created the perfect New Year's party because you love that holiday, but reveling on December 31 may just be something that delights you, even if you have no particular skill in party giving.

In the third column, list what you see as needing to be done in your community, your environment, or the place where you want to live. This could be a serious concern, like seeing your block cleared of trash, or a lighter one such as having more people attend the youth symphony orchestra performances that you adore.

Now comes the time to pick out some combinations that you love. Pick one from the resources column, one from the passions column, and one from the needs column. First, see what might logically go together. Then stretch your imagination by picking randomly.

PART III

Changes in Relationships

Men and women's differing approaches to handling change are often the cause of misunderstandings in relationships, even when intentions are good. In Chapter 9, you'll meet two couples who benefited from understanding the gender differences that occur during the changes of a marriage. In Chapter 10, you'll see the challenges of dating and courtship through the lens of gender change styles. Chapter 11 covers the change challenges of children and parents.

The Changes of Marriage and Divorce

THE ONE THING WE KNOW ABOUT MARRIAGE IS THAT IT'S FULL OF change. When you marry another person, you're going to have to learn just about everything anew: from what to do when you find the toothpaste squeezed from the bottom, to how to jointly manage finances when your money style is different from your partner's.

Living with another person isn't easy. It's the biggest change that most people face in early life. Making marriage into a loving and fulfilling experience requires a careful understanding of the way men and women cope with change.

Most people tend to marry relatively early in life—most often in their twenties or early thirties. However, not many individuals at this stage of life have strong change management skills. Worse yet, many people have not yet developed good communication skills with the opposite sex. It surely is a challenge when a young married man is confronted for the first time with his wife's menstrual difficulties, or when a young wife wonders why her new husband is lounging around in his underwear watching sports. It wasn't at all like this when he was bringing her flowers and concentrating on showing her his best behavior.

One secret to a successful marriage is to understand how your spouse handles change. The other secret is to understand how you handle change. If a couple can do this, they have a much better chance at staying together in a happy union.

The Story of Deborah and Mike

As a young married couple, Deborah and Mike were deeply in love, but they quickly found they approached change differently. Luckily, they were able to learn from each other and improve their understanding of each other's change style.

As a man, Mike was most comfortable being direct. For him that was the correct course of action. Deborah could easily have misinterpreted Mike's actions because, as a woman, she has a very different approach to dealing with change. She needed to be closer to her feelings and to talk difficulties over with others. Mike could have easily misinterpreted this as procrastination.

Both Mike and Deborah wanted the same result. They both wanted a happy and successful marriage. As is natural for a man and a woman, Mike and Deborah took very different roads to this goal, but they both finally arrived at the same place. They made the change work for them. In looking at their early difficulties after getting married, we will be able to show you how women and men make change work successfully for them.

Deborah was an early bird. She liked to get up at 6 A.M. and go to the gym. Mike was a night person. As a writer, a perfect day for him was to sleep until 11 A.M. At ten that night, he would be ready to charge out and go for pizza. By that time Deborah was exhausted.

This was a big change from their courtship when they did everything together.

Deborah couldn't understand why Mike lazed around in bed all morning every weekend. Mike couldn't understand why she didn't want to go out every evening. She'd been eager to go out when they were dating. How were they going to change the situation? They were worried that their marriage was off on the wrong foot.

Simple differences like these can cause many marriages to run up on the rocks quickly. But dealing with change in the right way can add spice back into a relationship.

Without time to develop skills for coping with change and not yet understanding what worked well for each of them, Deborah dealt with the changes in her routine, as she was accustomed to doing. She talked with her friends, did some research on the Internet, and decided that she and Mike should talk about how their lives had changed after the wedding.

> Simple differences cause many marriages to run up on the rocks.

Mike, on the other hand, thought he had the problem solved. During the week he felt that he deserved to sleep in until right before he had to leave for work, but on weekends, he would meet Deborah for brunch one Saturday a month.

This solution didn't impress Deborah very much. She was upset because when she got married, she thought Mike would change and start going to the gym with her. If Mike really loved her, she thought he'd get up to be with her early in the morning. Deborah wanted intimacy and expected Mike to need the same thing.

Mike for his part couldn't figure out why Deborah was nagging him already. Before they got married, she just went to the gym by herself and everything was fine. No complaints.

Why doesn't she just get her gym bag and go? he wondered. Mike wanted independence, and he expected Deborah to want it too.

If Deborah and Mike wanted to avoid a conflict in their marriage, they had to successfully manage the three important steps of the change in their relationship.

Saying Goodbye to the Past

The solution for Deborah and Mike turned out to be that they both had to acknowledge that the single life was behind them. There would be parts of that life they wanted to keep, as well as parts they needed to give up. Until they went through the ritual of mourning for what's lost (the freedom, excitement, and illusion of dating), they would have a hard time growing into the joys of marriage.

Both had to acknowledge that with marriage, the freedom of living alone was over. It meant that for the first time there was another person in the apartment who would sometimes be doing things contrary to what the other one wanted. They also had to realize that if the other person always wanted exactly what they wanted, it would be pretty boring.

The bachelor party is a ritual in our society, in which the groom is expected to say goodbye to carousing with the boys. It is the signal to the new husband that things from here on out will be different, so say goodbye to looking at other women. But there are other adjustments to be made to the realities of day-to-day living. Both Deborah and Mike soon found themselves bothered by the way married life called upon them to adjust.

For example, Deborah felt uncomfortable being around her new husband without dressing up. After all, she reasoned, when they had been courting, had always seen her in her best outfits, or at least in designer jeans. Now, she worried that

Mike would lose interest in her if she looked sloppy around the house. She decided to look good any time Mike was around. It took a little effort, but she started wearing better clothes around the house. Deborah decided to mourn the loss of being able to lounge around in her old sweats by making a ceremonial trip to The Gap.

Well, that helped. But there was still the problem of finding someone to share her feelings about the happenings of her day-to-day life. Mike didn't seem interested in the details of her day. He'd listen for a little bit but then turn on the television. "I'm listening," he'd say, "I just want to check out how the Mets did today. I'll mute it when the commercials come on." On the other hand, his feelings were hurt if she spent much time on the phone.

Before she married, Deborah was on the phone with her girlfriends or mother every day. But Mike objected when she was on the phone a lot.

Deborah at first thought she had to take her mother's advice and find a way that she and Mike could exercise together. "That will give you a time when you can talk," her mother reasoned. "And he'll be happier if he's also doing something else at the same time."

We agree with that advice because most men do multitask more easily than women and have much less of a need than women to talk about the details of life.

However, we disagreed with the advice that Deborah's mother went on to give. "Marriage," her mother said, "is more full of compromises for the woman." Deborah thought about that for a while and decided to try another way before she took that advice.

During change, women often make the mistake of thinking more about others' needs than their own. We advise that women be particularly sensitive to their own needs and that they be aware of their need to build their sense of self (as in Brock Change Skill 5, *Self-Sense*). This is generally more important for women than men.

Mike's first reaction was anger and frustration when he thought he was being asked to give up the extra sleep he felt he deserved after a hard week's work. It's a common male mistake during the first step of change not to sort out in his mind what to keep and what to let go.

Mike believed he had more than compromised by agreeing to a Saturday brunch once a month. This action showed Deborah that he loved her and wanted to make the marriage work, right?

What he needed to do was to be clear in his mind what he was giving up and what he was going to insist on keeping from his old life. Then, he must give up his natural tendency during Change Step 1, *Say Goodbye*, not to talk about it or be open to other points of view. This is difficult for most men.

Once he heard about the three change steps and the masculine difficulties with Change Step 1, Mike decided to work hard on communicating with Deborah by telling her what he needed but also by listening to her needs as well. So when she approached him with a way to get through the Middles, he agreed to at least consider it.

This proved to be a new insight for Mike. Once he saw the steps of change, he embraced the concept and understood it as a process to get through. As a man, he liked the structure and direct approach. What he needs to do is remind himself that it's okay to spend a little time saying goodbye to his single life, deciding what's important for him to keep and what he can let go of. He also needs to remember to talk with Deborah while he's doing it, listening to her needs and struggles to say goodbye to her single life, too.

The Middles

The Middles are when there's still one foot in the old way of life while the other one is ready to take the next step. This is the second change step, which happens after you know and accept that you'll need to do things differently. It's messy, like a bird's molting, and you want to get through it fast.

Mike asked that Deborah change her routine so that they could have at least one late evening "date" every week. His suggestion for *Moving Through the Middles* was to have a Tuesday night "date" for an entire month to focus on how they were doing in managing the conflict. They agreed to do it for only a month because Mike didn't like the idea of getting into the "touchy-feely stuff." But to make Deborah happy, he went along with the program. Here he was choosing to do the right thing for their relationship by setting up a temporary structure to get through the Middles fast.

For their regular Tuesday meetings, they agreed to these ground rules:

- To absolutely guarantee that when one is talking, the other listens 100 percent
- To stay on the topic for at least ninety minutes
- During the conversation, neither one walks away or mentally withdraws

These are absolute essentials in coming to a workable next step. If each person in the relationship is willing to give undivided attention to the other person, the chances of solving the problem goes way up. It helped that both realized that men don't look at the person they're listening to all the time, not nearly so much as women do. Mike made more of an effort to look at Deborah. She tried not to take it personally when he looked out the window occasionally while they were talking.

But remember, these are not summit meetings. Not all things can be expected to be resolved favorably at one time. They are more like knitting sessions, where a solution takes shape gradually as the threads of a solution are slowly woven together.

Mike acknowledged Deborah's need for companionship in the morning. She had examined her needs and felt this was something she really needed at least once in a while. But Mike didn't want to feel trapped into her schedule. So one Saturday a month, he agreed to get up an hour earlier so he could have brunch with Deborah after her workout. Mike is practicing Brock Change Skill 4, *Flexibility*. And it worked! If Deborah knows she's going to meet Mike, she doesn't feel lonely and abandoned.

The Middles are messy, and you want to get through them fast.

This couple got through the difficult Middles by creating a temporary fix, the Tuesday night "date" and the once-a-month Saturday brunch, to help them keep the marriage going while they were both adapting to the change. It felt uncomfortable. They recognized that the Middles were going to be hard, so they were simply tried to stay together, which they did successfully.

Start a New Beginning

The third and last change step occurs when you have a clear vision of the future. A new solution is better than a compromise. The latter too often makes one party feel like he or she's given up too much.

For Mike and Deborah, *New Beginnings* started when he started to think of new ways to celebrate Saturday brunch and began to learn how to cook and prepare an excellent brunch.

With a new idea, Deborah suggested late-night pizza Fridays and began asking friends to join them.

Change Lessons from Deborah and Mike

1. Bring your feelings of loss out into the open, and express concern for each other. Be specific about what each of you misses from the old life. Be sure you successfully complete Change Step 1, *Say Goodbye*, in terms of the past.
2. To her benefit, and despite advice from her mother, Deborah didn't listen to the little voice that told her she had to change something that was important to her to make the marriage work. The lesson here is to improve your Brock Change Skill 5, *Self-Sense*.
3. Mike didn't just plunge in and insist that he was entitled to sleep in after a hard week of work. The lesson here is to be sure you improve your Brock Change Skill 4, *Flexibility*.
4. Move quickly through the Middles period of change, and come up with a new ritual to symbolize your new beginnings. Use what you've learned about Change Steps 2 and 3.

Successful Change Management Following Failure

Angela and Byron, a similar couple, faced the same issues early in their marriage. We trace their marriage history from the beginning to the time they decided to call it quits. They hadn't learned the secrets of how the other gender manages change. But then a friend shared the ideas behind this book with them. We'll show you how they used their own individual version of the Brock Method to deal with their divorce productively.

Angela and Byron had a different experience managing the changes of marriage. They were married at the same time as Mike and Deborah. However, the course of their marriage ran very differently. Byron also was a night owl, and Angela was a lark. But he felt entitled to sleeping in on weekends and got angry when Angela wanted to talk about it. She started to criticize him for his "laziness." That just made him defensive about his sleeping habits.

Other issues started coming up. At first they were small. Angela didn't seem to get the symbolism of the presents Byron gave her. What would a wire statue of a couple have to do with her? Byron had meant it as a symbol of his love for her, which he found hard to express in words.

She reached out to her family and friends for support, but marriage to Byron hadn't been a popular choice, so she didn't get much support from them.

When her office moved to a more distant location, she didn't get home until after 7 P.M. At that time, she just wanted to eat a quick dinner, get ready for the next morning when she had to get up five, and be in bed by 10 P.M. For Byron, the evening was just starting, so he began going out to the neighborhood bar.

At first, he stayed home to at least say hello to Angela, but then he stopped even bothering. She seemed so distant that it hardly mattered anyhow.

When Angela's employers offered her an assignment in Asia, they decided to call it quits on the marriage.

What made the difference between Mike and Deborah's successful marriage and Angela and Byron's failure? First of all, Mike and Deborah took the time to acknowledge what each was losing with marriage. Angela and Byron heard only the Hollywood fantasy that marriage was bliss. When they didn't fulfill each other's fantasies, trouble was brewing.

When Byron tried to fix the problem by taking the action of a special, loving present for Angela, she criticized what he'd chosen. When she talked about her feelings of frustration, Byron, her friends, and family couldn't hear her. Angela and Byron never got past the first step of adapting to the changes in their marriage.

Angela did better the second time. She is a beautiful, bright, and optimistic woman, and the failed marriage taught her she'd have to change something about herself. She managed the double change of divorce and moving by first of all acknowledging what she had lost. She thought she might at least try working through the three change steps.

Saying Goodbye to the Past

Angela used the time on the long flight to Asia to make a list of what she was giving up with the divorce from Byron.

Some of the things on her list were the companionship she had by just having another person in her home, the sex life she shared with Byron, (though she had to say neither one of those had been very robust), and the security she had felt that came from being a married woman.

She considered the other good things too. Though it had been a while, she thought with pleasure about the times when Byron had made her laugh. He was a terrific cook.

But Angela was convinced that the time to say goodbye had finally come. She decided she would make a ritual goodbye to her marriage by having her engagement diamond reset into an attractive dinner ring.

As she landed in Hong Kong, Angela thought to herself that she should have mourned the absence of laughter from her marriage a long time ago. She found a way to replace it.

Get Through the Middles Fast

One thing Angela made a vow to do was to find a place for laughter in her new life. She knew the first few months were going to be tough in a new city, so she decided to put a couple of temporary measures in place. First of all, she agreed she would talk with her best friend twice a week on the phone even though the long distance charges were high. And she decided to do a "Pleasures from Asia" newsletter by e-mail every week to her Christmas card e-mail list of over a hundred people. The tone would be upbeat and light.

> Find a place for laughter in your new life.

She also wrote herself eight letters to be opened every Friday night for two months about why she was making this move. She talked about the job opportunity and the chance to grow by exploring a totally new culture.

She made up a sign to put on her bathroom mirror about what she expected to gain in the new experience. Also, she decided to give herself a reward of fresh flowers every week for experiencing her new, single life with enthusiasm. Angela got through the Middles with flying colors.

Start a New Beginning

Angela is starting her new life in Asia. We'll hear more about her in the next chapter and about how she is managing the changes of dating.

Change Lessons from Angela on Navigating Change Step 1

1. Accept the reality of emotional losses. (Brock Change Skill 3, *Emotional Resilience*).
2. Acknowledge what you lost, being sure to have compassion for yourself. (Change Step 1, *Say Goodbye*).

3. Create a symbol of what you have lost. (Change Step 1, *Say Goodbye*).

4. Keep clear about your goals. (Brock Change Skill 1, *Personal Vision*).

5. Reward yourself for risk-taking and acknowledge your small successes. (Brock Change Skill 4, *Flexibility*).

6. As you go into Change Step 2, *Move Through the Middles*, make a concerted effort to incorporate laughter and fun into your life. (Brock Change Skill 3, *Emotional Resilience*).

The Male Perspective

Byron stayed in their old house. Not many men make this choice, but Byron felt that staying in a familiar place gave him some stability during this time of great change in his life. The day Angela left, he looked at his life and decided to take some new directions in his life. He was thirty-five years old and he needed to make some better choices in his life. Now was his chance, he reasoned. He was free for the first time in years. He could do anything he wanted. A good friend introduced him to our concept of improving his change skills. He took it on with gusto.

Creating a Personal Vision

First Byron thought about what he wanted his life to be. He quickly decided on two areas where he wanted to concentrate: his dating life and his career. He had been working as a high security clearance engineer at a large multinational organization. He liked the people he worked with, but he'd been there for more than a decade. It was time for a change.

He started with what he really liked, what gave him the most pleasure.

What Byron was using was the middle column of the Mix 'n' Match Tool, passions. There's a copy of this tool at the end of Chapter 8. It's a way to help you create your own personal vision. The first column is your strengths, the middle column is what you're passionate about, and the last column is the places where there's a need for what you can do.

What Byron really liked was the idea of being his own boss. He was an excellent engineer and manager. He had often thought that there was a need in his region for an employment agency that specialized in chemical engineers who were qualified to work on high-security projects. He had a large set of contacts from the work he'd been doing and from his active role in his professional association.

Byron's vision became clear, and he made the first step of managing change. Like most men, Byron felt better taking direct action. He started TempChemSecure on the side, but as requests started coming in, he was able to go full-time after a year.

Reframing

Byron's biggest insight came in the way a friend helped him to look at his marriage. Byron felt it was a failure and, as a result, tried not to talk about it and to hide his anger. The friend suggested he look at the five years he spent being married as a period of calm in his life when he was able to concentrate on building his career skills and contacts.

Once Byron realized how much time dating took, he accepted that marriage had allowed him time to work with few interruptions. Angela had also taken care of many of the household responsibilities. He was amazed at how much time he spent at mindless chores like laundry and cleaning now that he was divorced—time that would have taken him away from developing his career during his marriage.

Now that he was single, Byron was able to reframe his thinking about his divorce from Angela. He saw their five-year marriage as an experience in his life that had many pleasant memories and good times, but one that, like many things, finally had to end. His marriage was not a failure. It was one period of his life that was full of memories and lessons for the future that was now over. Byron made a habit of looking forward, not back.

> Reframe your thinking about divorce.

Emotional Resilience

When he'd been dating before getting married, Byron had been pretty impatient. He liked to move quickly out of any relationship that didn't work out. Speaking of passions, he knew he really wanted a woman, and perhaps even many women, in his life. The last year of his marriage had been very empty. He felt angry and cynical about women.

Byron decided to start acting like the attractive, charming man that he was. He remembered his ability to get almost any woman to laugh. As friends introduced him to eligible women and he could see they had fun with him, his anger slowly diminished. Byron started to put his marriage in the past as he enjoyed the company of many bright and attractive women.

Flexibility

Byron decided he would open up to a wider range of women who he thought would be partners. He had always favored the beautiful and rejected any woman who didn't look like a model. He set aside a month in which he would ask every woman out who seemed interesting, no matter what she looked like. He set an "only one date required" rule, but he really tried to be open to different types of women.

Sense of Self

Looking back on it, Byron had to admit that Angela had really done him a favor by opting out of the marriage when she got her assignment to Asia. He'd thought he'd been pretty sure who he was in his twenties. But now as he charted a personal vision and reframed his situation, he found he had grown into a much more interesting person.

Change Lessons from Byron

1. Create a personal vision combining strengths and passions (Brock Change Skill 1, *Personal Vision*).
2. Reframe. Byron was able to reframe his divorce from being a personal failure to being an accomplishment that had lasted many years and had provided him with many life lessons (Brock Change Skill 2, *Reframing*).
3. Act as if you are the success you want to be, and improve your Brock Change Skill 3, *Emotional Resilience*.
4. In a period of change, look at the things that make you angry. This helped Byron to be more flexible in dating eligible women (Brock Change Skill 4, *Flexibility*).
5. Take change as a chance to learn, and improve your Brock Change Skill 5, *Self-Sense*.

Remembering Our Differences

Men and women can benefit greatly in a marriage or divorce by remembering how different we are in dealing with change. Men don't realize that their direct approach to change can threaten women. It is true that the action-oriented solutions that men naturally follow when coping with change usually work well three-quarters of the time for them. But men also need to understand that women can misinterpret direct outward action and feel as if their needs are being overlooked. Men in marriage need to reassure their spouses that they value their different brand of coping with change.

Women, on the other hand, naturally move toward a more thoughtful approach to change. They need to reach out to others, talk about feelings, and research what the best solution might be. Men may misinterpret this as procrastination or indecision. It's not. This is the feminine approach to coping with change. It frequently produces a less structured and more creative solution.

Men and women who have a successful marriage will have had many chances to cope with change. By recognizing how the other gender goes through the three change steps and the importance of developing the five Brock change skills, the likelihood for a successful relationship increases. Heaven knows, it's difficult enough to deal with all of the things life throws at you every year, but at least we can get along better in our relationships with the opposite gender by realizing that each has inborn strengths to deal with change.

Both men and women need to understand each gender has a unique approach to three essential steps of change: *Say Goodbye, Move Through the Middles,* and *New Beginnings.*

Each of us needs to recognize and encourage our mate in the five Brock change skills: *Personal Vision, Reframing, Emotional Resilience, Flexibility,* and *Self-Sense.*

Mike managed to overcome his natural resistance and did this. Because of that he is now happier in his relationship with Deborah. He understands her better, too.

In addition, Deborah feels that by going through the three change steps and talking about each of them with Mike, they're closer. They've decided to make the Brock Method for improving their skills in handling change a part of their lives.

Angela and Byron are still friends despite their divorce. Both firmly believe they now have richer lives because they better understand how men and women have different ways of handling change.

Chapter 10

The Challenges of Dating and Courtship

WE KNOW THAT DATING IS FULL OF HIGHS AND LOWS. REGARDLESS of whether the eventual intent is marriage, if there is a desire to have a relationship with another person, there will have to be changes on both sides. No matter what age, there are challenges.

One way to guarantee you'll be more successful in dating is to understand how the opposite gender handles change.

The differences in how men and women perceive things have long been observed through humor. Here's a recent story circulating the Internet.

"A language instructor was explaining to her adult class that in French, nouns, unlike their English counterparts, are grammatically designated as masculine or feminine. 'House' in French is feminine, '*la maison.*' 'Pencil' in French is masculine, '*le crayon.*' One puzzled student asked, 'What gender is a computer?' The teacher didn't know and the word wasn't in her French dictionary.

"So for fun she split up the class into two groups, appropriately enough by gender, and asked them to decide whether 'computer' should be a feminine or masculine noun. Both groups were required to give four reasons for their recommendations.

"The men's group decided that computers should definitely be feminine *(la computer)* for the following reasons:

1. No one but their creator understands their internal logic.
2. The native language that they employ to communicate with each other is incomprehensible to everyone else.
3. Even the smallest mistakes are stored in long-term memory for possible later retrieval.
4. As soon as you make a commitment to one, you find yourself spending half your paycheck on accessories for it.

"The women's group, however, decided that computers should be masculine, because:

- In order to get their attention, you have to turn them on.
- They have a lot of data but they are still clueless.
- They are supposed to help you solve problems, but half the time they are the problem.
- As soon as you commit to one, you realize that if you'd waited a little longer, you could have gotten a better model."

In other words, for all of their similarities, men and women perceive the world quite differently.

This chapter introduces you to David and Celeste. It also fills you in on how new divorcée Angela started a dating life in her new community. We also find out what happened to her ex-husband, Byron.

The Research: What He Said; What She Said

David and Celeste were at the beginning at their dating relationship when we met them. In their early thirties, they both expressed interest in marriage and a family but were having difficulty meeting the right partner and sustaining a long-term relationship.

"In dealing with change, women tend to use a more emotion-driven approach, while men use more mind-driven ones. Women seem to be more flexible when change takes place," says David, an MBA student who works at a large bank. "Women also seem to need more support when experiencing change. My last girlfriend always seemed to be on the phone, talking with her friends."

When he met Celeste at a professional association meeting, they immediately hit it off. They both were hard workers and shared a passion for tennis. Both had recently broken off long-term relationships and were a bit wary of staring a new one.

"Men," exclaimed Celeste, "just see things differently than women. They want it one way, their way, and don't seem to be able to hear what a woman says. I like strong men, but it's too easy for me to be sympathetic and just go along with what he wants. Then I lose track of my needs. Only my female friends seem to be able to let me be me." She was attracted to David, though, and was impressed with the way he listened to her.

During change, women are more likely to consult others, looking for support from friends, and seeking others' advice before taking action. It is important that men see this as an effective and quite natural female reaction to change, rather than a hesitation that can be viewed by a man as a sign of weakness and doubt.

This desire to seek out advice from others that women share is reflected in the concept of this book's title. A woman traveling somewhere will often want to be told what the guideposts are along the way, and she will usually be willing to stop and ask for further help in getting to her destination. A man is more likely to consult a map and "head east," determined to get there on his own. The reluctance of men to stop to ask for directions is the subject of a lot of jokes, but it does in fact have a basis in real differences between men and women.

When a man understands that his date or fiancée will frequently react to change in a very different way than he would but can successfully reach the same destination in her own way, a stronger relationship between them can develop.

Until he understood the female approach, David was perplexed that Celeste wanted him to start spending weekends with her in her new country home. She'd done a lot of research to find the best area for a weekend home and wanted David to take advantage of it too. He liked his city apartment and didn't want to give up his weekend sports get-togethers with his friends. Celeste reasoned that living together on weekends would be a good way to find out if she and David were compatible. She wanted to change her city weekend routine for a summer of weekends of sun and fun.

David, realizing that this is the way Celeste as a woman is programmed to change, agreed to try it out for one weekend a month. However, he asked that she spend one weekend in the city, so they can be together and he could also see his friends.

Saying Goodbye to the Past

Both David and Celeste got off to a better start because they were able to understand each other's change style as a man and as a woman. They also had each been through enough unsuccessful relationships that they knew a new approach was needed.

David came to the conclusion that getting into a serious relationship with Celeste was going to require him to give up some time with his friends. He listened to Celeste and realized one thing she really liked about him was his ability to listen, so he decided to emphasize this.

In going through this first stage of change, it's as important to identify what you will give up as it is to know what you will not sacrifice. This time Celeste decided that she was going to maintain her individuality and spend some time making sure she was getting what she needed. She realized she'd been too accommodating in past relationships and ended up breaking off because she'd felt compromised.

The Middles

The trial period that David and Celeste worked out— spending one weekend a month at her country place with her friends—is an example of a temporary structure put into place to get to Change Step 3, *New Beginnings*. Not all couples make it through the process of *Moving Through the Middles* of dating and courtship, but David and Celeste used the time to understand each other better. They played a lot of tennis and even hooked up with a doubles league. But Celeste also entered the singles championship ladder at her club and was runner-up. David came and cheered her on.

Celeste was smart enough to realize that, as a man, David just needed to jump in and do something, and that this was a concrete action even though it required David to be on her turf. She was especially sensitive that she not spend most of her time with her friends, but actually balanced out time with David alone and with David's friends. They each also decided to spend two weekends a month apart, giving each time to spend with their respective groups. This helped Celeste feel that she was better able to keep hold of her individuality but also to explore a serious relationship with David.

New Beginnings

It's been a year now. David and Celeste are still together. They spend more time together now. The talk of marriage is in the air. Celeste is spending time researching wedding plans. It's fun to be able to talk with her friends about them.

David is enjoying the time with Celeste, but he may have a major promotion at his job, so there will be more change. He's decided he wants to talk about the possibilities of where he could live together with Celeste. One thing they've decided is that any place they move will have to have a nearby tennis court because they have enjoyed playing together so much.

Change Lessons from David and Celeste

1. Express your dissatisfaction with the way past relationships have gone, and decide the specific ways you each will act differently this time (Brock Change Skill 1, *Personal Vision*).

2. Celeste told David she especially appreciated his listening ability and how unusual she found that in a man. This is an important part of the Brock Change Skill 2, *Reframing*. David worked to increase his listening when he was with Celeste.

3. In saying goodbye to her old life, Celeste was able to identify not only what was going away, but also what she needed to hold on to. In her case, she needed to tone down her natural inclination to accommodate others during change. She needed to learn how to

make adjustments without losing her *Self-Sense* (Brock Change Skill 5).

4. Make time for a transition period, the Middles, which takes pressure off the relationship (Change Step 2).

Starting Dating Anew

We're going to continue the story of Angela and Byron, the couple who separated at the end of the last chapter. They did divorce, and Angela was left with the change challenge of starting up a new life in Hong Kong, where her job had taken her. She took one very successful pathway to dating.

Her actions reflect the feminine style of handling change.

Angela started using the Brock Method to grow with change during the move. She was intrigued enough to see if it might help in getting her started dating in Hong Kong and cope with the changes involved in forming a successful relationship with the opposite sex.

Just as many women get themselves into their best physical shape when they go into the dating market, Angela decided she would also use the Brock Method to pump up her change skills.

Creating a Personal Vision

Angela thought about what she wanted in a dating relationship. She decided that she wasn't ready for a second marriage yet. Instead, she wanted to spend a couple of years dating and getting to know different types of partners.

She asked a single girlfriend to come over Sunday afternoon so she could go through the Mix 'n' Match Tool for dating. She jokingly called the friend, May, her "dating coach." Angela said, "Well, I've got a personal trainer to help me get my body in optimum shape, why not a dating coach?"

The two women listed Angela's strengths as a prospective date: She is attractive, young (twenty-eight), intelligent, easy to talk with, and likes many different types of people. Her apartment is small but centrally located, and she enjoys entertaining. She has an interesting job and unusual hobbies including billiards, opera, and photography. The kinds of men she wanted to date would be single and have a good sense of humor.

May pushed her further in specifying exactly who she'd enjoy going out with. Wisely, she said, "You can be so broad that everyone qualifies and the guy doesn't feel special to be chosen."

They started to laugh when they came up with the picture of her ideal date walking in carrying a camera with a billiard cue in his hand, singing an aria from *Madame Butterfly*. "But," May said, "let's just spend a few minutes figuring out where you might meet this person." They decided to search out photography exhibits, opera performances, and places that had billiard tables.

It was a plan and certainly an enjoyable Sunday afternoon. Angela also felt she'd gained a better sense of herself by going through the exercise (Brock Change Skill 5, *Self-Sense*).

Reframing

In many ways, Angela reframed the way she approached dating by "hiring" May to be her dating coach. May also agreed to be her reframing buddy and available to reframe the dating search and dates as they happen. Angela went into the situation expecting to have fun and learn about herself, but she was also serious about finding a partner. This was a very different frame than the one she used when she met Byron when she was right out of college.

They also used the reframing tool to help put dating disasters into perspective. At first Angela was horrified when she went to an Ivy League club mixer. She'd dressed in an attractive business suit, as had most of the others. But the men were largely gathered around a young woman in a very low-cut dress. She and May just had a laugh over that one.

| Put dating disasters into perspective.

Emotional Resilience

Angela worked hard on emotional resilience. She knew she was stressed from several big changes (divorce, moving, job transfer) happening all at once. So she took special care to observe the three Brock Method tips for increasing her emotional resilience: balancing her life, training mentally and physically, and planning recovery time.

It was particularly hard for her not to just spend 100 percent of her time on her job. Even though she was basically doing the same thing as she had done in her old job, the people were all different. However, she insisted on time to build up friendships, to get integrated with the community, and to keep up with her family and friends at home.

Angela likes to take special care to watch her health. It was a luxury, she realized, for her to hire a personal trainer. But she thought it was necessary for her sanity, so she went ahead and did it.

She and May built a recovery period into her dating program. She decided that she'd do date-directed activities three times a week. Either she'd have a date or go to an activity where she'd have a good chance of meeting the man she sketched out with the Mix 'n' Match Tool. However, she and May agreed to keep Sunday afternoons open so they could kick back, talk about their adventures, and laugh or cry.

"Hiring" a coach for dating and continuing to meet with her is a typically feminine approach to change. For this enterprise, Angela and May behaved like their brains have been wired for socialization during change. A man would not be likely to want to talk about his dating experiences with another man, nor would he reveal his feeling about the frustrations of dating.

Flexibility

Building flexibility involves practice, so Angela decided she would keep varying the ways she reached out to find a dating partner. Sometimes she went out to events like photography exhibits or the opera, where she might meet a man interested in those subjects. Other times she gave small dinner parties in her apartment with the new friends she was meeting.

It was an idea from the Brock Method—that of breaking down big tasks into small ones—that enabled Angela to meet the man she still dates today.

One Friday night, Angela had a workmate sign her up to go to the Governor's Ball for the Sydney Opera Company that was visiting for a performance that weekend. It was a formal affair, and Angela found a dress that was right.

However, as the time approached, she started getting cold feet. She was tired from a hard week at work. Fighting her desire to quit, she remembered the tips about building flexibility by "breaking down" and rewarding "small wins" in a tough project struck a chord.

Angela said, "I could do that. What I'll do is just take it a step at a time and reward myself after each one."

She told herself that after the hair and makeup appointment she could have a nice dinner of homemade soup she had in the refrigerator. She did that.

Now, she told herself, my next step is to get my dress on and take a cab to the ball. The fear really started to build. She made an agreement with herself that if she was really too tired when she got to the ball, she could just turn around and go home.

Arriving at the ball, Angela screwed up her courage, saying to herself, "I'm here. I might as well go in and check it out." She did and promised herself she would stay to get one drink.

It was worse than she anticipated. The room was huge, with very masculine decorations including a stuffed moose and warthog heads on the walls. There were a number of people there, but everyone was seated at small table either alone, in couples, or groups.

She got the drink. Then she decided that all she had to do was walk the length of the room once to see if there was anyone she knew. She did, and there wasn't.

With her last ounce of courage she said to herself, "Just pick a likely single man. Ask to sit down with him a minute, drink your drink, and leave."

She did that. The man she chose turned out to be very nice, and she ended up talking with him the rest of the evening. As they walked out to say good night, they passed a billiard table, and he asked her if she played.

Sense of Self

The Mix 'n' Match Tool was useful to Angela in building up her sense of self. She was glad she wrote down her strengths. She went back to that piece of paper when she'd had a particularly challenging dating experience.

She also became more assertive in telling others that she wanted to meet eligible men. She even gave them the picture of the ideal man she'd like to meet.

Change Lessons from Angela
1. Use dating as a chance to get to know yourself better (Brock Change Skill 1, *Personal Vision*).
2. "Hire" a coach to help you through the changes that dating entails (Brock Change Skill 3, *Emotional Resilience*).
3. The Mix 'n' Match tool is a great help when it comes to reinforcing your sense of self (Brock Change Skill 5) and getting a clear picture of what you want.
4. Being assertive is essential when it comes to asking others to help you get what you want (Brock Change Skill 5, *Self-Sense*).
5. Dating is difficult. Celeste rewarded herself at each new step she took (Brock Change Skill 4, *Flexibility*).

The Male Perspective

Let's move now to Angela's ex-husband, Byron. Remember that he's now thirty-six years old, living in their old home. He's been able to make his dream of running a company come alive and is in his first year of full-time operation of his new company, which specializes in finding chemical engineers qualified to work on high-security projects.

He's done the work of reframing his marriage from being a failure to being a part of his life with pleasant memories and good times. He's been able to be more patient about dating and not expecting Ms. Perfect to knock on his door. He's been dating sporadically, mostly through being fixed up with eligible women by friends. He's tried to be open, but hasn't really met anyone he has wanted to get serious with.

Now that work was getting a little more settled, Byron decided to take a Saturday evening and put together a plan for finding the right woman. He also decided to make whatever changes were necessary to have a successful dating relationship.

Creating a Personal Vision

Byron didn't really want to take time to go through the Mix 'n' Match Tool again. He thought he had a pretty good idea of what his personal vision was for his dating life. He wanted to meet an attractive, eligible woman who was interested in starting a family. She'd need to support him in his efforts to run a new business. It would also be great if she enjoyed late night parties and didn't mind if he slept in occasionally.

"But," Byron thought as he read about the need to think about what strengths he brought to a relationship, "what do I have to offer?" He still felt a little bruised after the divorce. He already started to practice being the attractive, charming man he was before the marriage. He looked at some of the strengths he had in business and thought they could also be strengths for a dating relationship. Why not look for a woman who appreciated the intelligence, loyalty, and passion he demonstrated in his business life?

Reframing

How could Byron look at the dating challenge in a creative way?

As a man, he thought, "I'll just multitask. I'll look for a dating relationship online, but I can also be networking for new clients and new talent." And that's what he did. Byron joined several online chat rooms. Some to had to do with dating, while other Web sites were to meet people in his area of occupation.

Three weeks later he had tens of resumes for his business and five e-mail addresses of women he wanted to follow up with for possible dates.

Emotional Resilience

Byron did buy in to the Brock Method strategy of strengthening emotional resilience by getting your body in shape physically. He'd been something of a workout nut before he was married, so he rejoined the gym and started going nearly every day.

He also like the idea of recovery time, so he decided to spend plenty of time getting to know each of the five women. Then, he thought, he'd plan a long weekend away from the whole scene when he could visit his sister and her children.

Flexibility

Byron was still using the "only one date required" approach, so he was practicing flexibility by extending himself to go out with women who didn't meet his criteria 100 percent.

He also decided he was going to change his usual dating approach of asking a woman out for a fancy dinner and then, after that one date, deciding if he wanted to continue seeing her. It was hard, but he decided to take it a little slower and start e-mail conversations with each of the five women. Then the opportunity to meet could flow a little more naturally out of the conversation that evolved.

Women, he started to notice, seem to take more time to get to know their dates. They enjoy having the early dates outside the stressful environment of a fancy (and expensive) dinner.

Sense of Self

As the e-mailing got started, Byron felt more comfortable showing some of himself to each of the women. He had an initial slow start with Julia because she told him she was definitely a morning person and usually didn't spend much time out partying after midnight. However, he was intrigued that she also had started her own business. He had to tell himself that he was on an adventure and had promised himself to be open to new kinds of people.

Byron and Julia finally met in person for a cup of coffee after five weeks of e-mailing. They did hit it off and have been dating for six months now. Some of their time is spent comparing notes about their respective businesses.

It turns out they both like having their own worlds. She's up and around in the early morning, while he has his own time late at night. How that might play into marriage and children is under discussion.

Byron is pleased to have met Julia, however, and realizes that without changing his approach to dating and understanding more of how women approach it, he never would have hooked up with her.

Change Lessons from Byron

1. Reframe the search phase of dating as an activity you can combine with something else (Brock Change Skill 2, *Reframing*).
2. Learn that creating a space for a new life is difficult (Brock Change Skill 3, *Emotional Resilience*).
3. Realize that happiness is not always what you expect (Brock Change Skill 2, *Reframing*).
4. Learn how the opposite gender copes with dating, and make changes from your usual approach (Brock Change Skill 4, *Flexibility*).

Remembering Our Differences

Men and women can benefit in dating situations if they remember how differently each gender approaches the changes that dating brings into life. Men don't realize that their decisive approach confuses women. With a woman, it's easier to feel comfortable in the stressful situation of dating if the man is willing to go slowly and get to know her as a person.

Women also need to understand that their approach of gathering in a group of friends and talking amongst themselves about the stresses of dating is not one that attracts men. It's better to define what you want, know what you have to give, and be assertive in seeking to talk with a number of men.

Both genders approach the change that dating brings in a different way. These methods work for them, but knowing how the opposite gender copes with dating can make it work even better. David and Celeste formed a solid relationship by helping each other through the first step of saying their good-byes to their old unattached lives, trying a new way to do things in the Middles, and talking about what they saw as their new beginning—that their relationship was going toward.

Angela and Byron showed how to use the five Brock change skills to make it through a major change—Angela with the Mix 'n' Match Tool in conjunction with her "dating coach" May, Byron in an informal way.

Ten Secrets of Dating and Courtship

For Women:	For Men:
1. Learn from your past relationships, and then say goodbye to them.	1. Listen, listen, listen.
2. Identify what it is you want from a relationship with the opposite sex and what you have to give.	2. Be clear on what you want from a woman and what you have to offer.
3. Define what you think romance is and let your partner in on it.	3. Ask her what she expects from a dating relationship.
4. Recognize that it's normal for him to act before talking.	4. Reframe past relationships as useful parts of your personal history.
5. Men have different time schedules than women in dating.	5. Recognize that she needs to talk with other people in her life and get their support.
6. Sometimes it's better just to follow his lead and then find out the reasons later.	6. It's more comfortable for her if you tell her why before acting.
7. It's difficult for him to talk about his feelings, and he doesn't like to do it.	7. Listening for a woman means undivided attention. Limit multitasking.
8. He wants to make you happy.	8. She wants to please you—perhaps too much.
9. He has a hard time predicting what you want.	9. She has a hard time figuring you out.
10. He needs to feel like he's free to make his own decisions.	10. She appreciates the fact that you're different from her.

Chapter 11

Change Challenges for Children and Parents

IN THIS CHAPTER, WE WILL APPLY OUR METHODS TO THE CHANGE challenges of children and parents. Relationships between any two people are complex, and this is even more the case with the three people involved in a parent/child relationship. That complexity only increases as the size of the family gets larger.

Initially, each of the parents is adapting to the change of having a new baby in the household. Then, as the child grows and perhaps others come, new and different change challenges emerge.

From the time the baby is new until he or she is ready to be leaving the nest, from managing your child to letting your grown children manage you, parenting means coping with change. Men have one way to do it; women have another way. Both are successful, and we can be even more successful if we understand the other gender's natural style.

Jose and Valerie were just beginning the challenges and joys of parenthood, but they quickly ran into problems. They were able to deal with the changes a new baby brought into their lives by using a few simple techniques, which we'll learn about in this chapter. We'll check in on Sheila to see how she's coping with change in raising her two teenage daughters.

Lastly we'll tell you the story of Lily and Leon, siblings who had come to that point in life at which their parents needed care. They are handling the change challenges posed by aging parents according to what's more natural for their genders.

In our many conversations with professionals from all around the country who specialize in human development, we found a deep concern for the struggles that men and women endure during their ordinary lives. Regina, a Ph.D. and an executive at a professional association, observed, "I see big differences in how men and women adapt to parenthood and working. Women need less structure and regulation."

This was indeed the fact with Jose and Valerie, one of the couples in our seminar group.

The Research: What He Said; What She Said

Jose had been working in the technology sector of a telephone company in Chicago and living in a suburb with his wife, Valerie. She had been teaching second grade in a nearby school since they married two years ago. Both wanted a family, so the initial response to her pregnancy was delight. But both knew their relationship would change.

Saying Goodbye to the Past

As a woman, Valerie went about going through the first step of change by saying goodbye to their carefree days of being a childless couple. This step is easier for most women, and for Valerie her changing body was also telling her things were going to be different.

Jose preferred to go on as usual. He was looking forward to being a father, but he thought that because they'd both planned and looked forward to the new baby, he'd just adjust naturally.

Many people are like that, expecting only negative changes to be difficult. Our research shows that positive changes require just as much adaptation.

Valerie was smart in knowing the ways of men and how they react to change. For most of them, Change Step 1, *Say Goodbye,* is something they'd just as soon skip. However, Valerie insisted that Jose sit down with her and talk about what changes they would make. One real concern was that Jose had an hour-and-a-half commute every day on the train. Added to that was his work schedule of ten-hour days, plus the paperwork he brought home. He wasn't really going to have much time for the new addition.

Together they did the How I Spend My Time Exercise in Chapter 8 to see if they should be thinking of ways to strengthen Jose's emotional resiliency. "Babies," Valerie pointed out, after talking with friends of hers who were new mothers, "are stressful, no matter how much joy they bring." When Jose saw in black and white that he was now spending 85 percent of his waking hours either at work or on his commute, he started to think of alternatives.

The Middles

Jose didn't really see how he could change his company; he'd been there two years and was on a fast track. However, he realized that Valerie was right, so he decided he would explore some temporary solutions. This step of adapting to change, the Middles, comes more naturally to men. The Middles usually is a temporary structure that is adopted until a permanent coping mechanism is in place.

Jose took the action of talking with his human resources director, explaining the situation and asking if there was any temporary job he could be assigned nearer his home for the next few years. The director was very agreeable. Within two weeks, she came up with a two-year assignment for Jose that involved running the information interchange depot for his employer, at a location that was within a five-minute commute of his home.

New Beginnings

Valerie was delighted with Jose's assignment. He actually was pleased to get the management experience. Once the baby came, he found he could occasionally sneak out for lunch hours to spend some time with his new son. Being on call twenty-four hours a day, seven days a week seemed a small price to pay. Besides, he was so close to the new office and also often awake at night due to his son's healthy lungs.

In this case, what Jose and Valerie had conceived as a temporary solution worked so well that it became permanent. The new beginning that they both wanted was for both of them to be able to spend time with the baby but also continue their jobs.

Change Lessons from Jose and Valerie

1. In a partnership, use the feminine strength of being able to *Say Goodbye* and then switch to the male strength of being able to start quickly *Moving Through the Middles* with direct action.
2. They learned that a major life change is a perfect time to check life balance, thus improving their skills in Brock Change Skill 3, *Emotional Resilience*.
3. It can come as a surprise that positive changes, too, have to be coped with (Brock Change Skill 2, *Reframing*).

The Female Perspective

Now let's hear from Sheila, a single mother who used her understanding of the five Brock change skills to move forward in her life. Sheila has made herself a model for her girls by creating a career that gives her time from 7:30 to 9:30 A.M. to devote to writing her novel. You'll also get the perspective of Sheila's teenage daughters to show how their mother's action has helped them increase their flexibility.

Creating a Personal Vision

Sheila always knew what she wanted to do with her life: to write the great American novel while providing a nurturing home for her daughters Joan (fifteen) and Crystal (thirteen). Sheila was a talented writer, with a flair for expressive prose, which wasn't appreciated at the nonprofit company where she'd been working in corporate communications.

She knew what she was good at and passionate about—writing and her children. The challenge was to find or create a place where she could do both. So, in creating her personal vision, the emphasis was on finding the place. She found it in that third column of the Mix 'n' Match Tool.

Sheila and her girls decided to make completing the Mix 'n' Match Tool a project, so they set aside a weekend and gathered poster board, markers, and old magazines to clip from.

What they came away with was an agreement that allowed Sheila to spend two hours a day for the next year writing so she could finish a draft of her novel to show publishers. That meant that Sheila would seek out a job that was more enriching and where she didn't have to start until late in the morning, around ten or so. Everyone had fun working with the art supplies. They put up the final "picture" in the living room.

The change meant that Crystal and Joan had to take on more of the responsibility of managing housework. The girls were willing to take on more of the household chores. Crystal volunteered to make breakfast and clean up the dishes in the morning. That way Sheila could get up and write from 7:30 A.M. to 9:30 A.M. Joan would start dinner preparations, expecting that Sheila wouldn't usually be home until seven in the evening.

We find that making an actual picture of your personal vision has magic to it. Many people feel awkward doing this, but we have been surprised at how often it comes true. This is easier for women to do.

Sheila was also smart in expressing trust in her girls to take on more responsibility. The initial step of change always feels awkward. The tendency is to clam up and want to do more of everything yourself.

Reframing

By thinking of a job as a part of her life in which she needed to be nurtured as well as one that needed to fit into her time requirements, Sheila had reframed the role of work in her life. Before, it had been a way to make as much money as she could to support herself and her children.

However, Sheila still needed to make money. As she looked at the want ads, she saw a situation that looked promising. It was teaching economically deprived high school children how to write. The program was funded and run out of her local school district. Even better, the hours were 10 to 6, exactly what Sheila needed. She interviewed for the job and was impressed with the quality of people administering the program. She also met a few of the children and thought they had interesting stories to tell. She was offered the job.

The salary was only 80 percent of what Sheila had been making. She decided to take the problem back to the household council and see what they could come up with as a creative solution.

Emotional Resilience

Sheila and her family had been practicing the Brock Method for building emotional resilience. They'd also worked hard to make their church a part of their lives. So when Sheila went to ask advice, the minister came up with an idea for a way to fill in the economic gap. One of the other parishioners was a part of a committee that worked to support and develop new artists in the community. They made select grants to people like Sheila who needed a loan to tide them over while they were heavily involved in their art.

Sheila continues to be amazed in her life when something good comes from an unexpected source. Many of us anticipate and worry about the bad things that will come from nowhere, but rarely do we anticipate the good things that also often come from a source not counted on.

Flexibility

Each of the three females in this family prided herself on her flexibility. In fact, women do find it easier both physically and mentally to try new ways. They had made a game out of finding new ways to do things. When Sheila convened the home council on her new job offer and the possible assistance of the Artist's Loan Program, the girls cheered "Go for it, Mom!" in unison.

Sense of Self

One of the best things Sheila believes she did to change her life was to join a Dream Team. It was a group of seven women, all coming from different walks of life. They'd come together through friends to support each other in their individual dreams.

They met monthly and shared progress on their dreams. Sheila started using not only the meetings but e-mail to keep her Dream Team up on her writing. She would send chapters for review. She got back lots of helpful hints and encouragement. This helped her start seeing herself as a practicing writer.

She recently revealed to them, "Last night it hit me! I always do my chores, this and that, and leave my dreams for last. Seems awfully self-destructive, doesn't it? I know my girls want me to do it, are supportive and will benefit the most by watching an adult *do* what she loves, so maybe I should follow their lead and believe in their mom." We agree. It's like the script you hear on an airplane, "In case of a problem with decompression, put your oxygen mask on first, then help the child beside you."

The team also helped her start acting as if she was a writer. She started outlining the proposal she would send out to publishers and agents. She laid out her plans in detail, learning that the more concrete you make your dream, the closer you are to making it happen.

Sheila used her concept of having many roles and many ways to look at work to help her brother in Texas, who had been stuck in a routine job at an Austin company. Through her encouragement, he's reignited his boyhood interest in photography and even manages to catch interesting shots on his way to and from work.

Change Lessons from Sheila

1. When change happens, communicate more often and make visible expressions of trust (Change Step 3, *New Beginnings*).
2. Think about work as a way to fulfill more than money needs, reframing its place in your life (Brock Change Skill 3, *Emotional Resilience*).

3. During times of change, ask for advice and help (Brock Change Skill 5, *Self-Sense*).
4. Anticipate good things happening (Brock Change Skill 5, *Self-Sense*).
5. Make your personal vision as concrete as possible (Brock Change Skill 1, *Personal Vision*), and talk about it to as many people as you can.
6. Finally, practice what you preach. Sheila makes her dreams a priority. Do the same, and your children will notice (Change Step 3, *New Beginnings*).

For each change challenge in the children and parent relationship, there's a male strategy and a female strategy. For example, when parents are faced with an empty nest, women are more likely to engage grown children in the network of family activities: a grandmother's birthday, a christening for a new grandchild. Men, on the other hand, tend to gravitate to helping grown children solve their life issues: what to do when laid off by a dot-com or how to network when relocated. In becoming a caretaker for elderly parents, the female strategy is to bring the parents into the home, under the woman's care. The male strategy is to find a team of caregivers to provide the parents with support.

Male and Female Approaches That Complement Each Other

Lily and Leon had different approaches to the situation of managing elderly parents.

As brother and sister, Lily and Leon had joint responsibility for making sure their parents, who lived in Hawaii, were taking care of themselves. Everything was going smoothly.

Lily, who lives in Connecticut with her husband and two daughters, visited twice a year, in the spring and the end of the year and whenever her business travel took her in that direction. Leon in San Francisco was able to plan trips every quarter. He was closer and as yet had no children.

Then Dad had a stroke, leaving him partially paralyzed. Things were going to have to change.

Say Goodbye

Lily and her mother took the more feminine approach and grieved mightily over the loss of independence that the paralysis was going to make on the household. Dad's outlook for survival was excellent, but he was going to have to use a wheelchair. He took it well, and soon was back to his optimistic, joking self.

Leon heard his father's assurances that everything was going to be okay. He headed back to his wife and job and expected his life not to change. It was Lily who insisted that the family address the issue of what changes needed to be made in their parents' living arrangement.

The Middles

It was Leon, in typical male style, who made the fast decision for action. He decided that his parents would have to move into a place where they could have nursing assistance. It would be too much for their mother to have to move their father several times a day. So Leon went back to Hawaii and searched for senior care facilities and put a deposit on one.

"I've solved the problem," he said when he called Lily from Hawaii. "What!" she replied getting anxious and angry. "I hope you haven't just acted without consulting any of us." As the truth came out, Leon hadn't even involved his mother and father in the decision. They of course were reluctant to leave their home.

Lily was steaming. "I know you're anxious to get the situation under control," she said, "but we need to talk about this with everyone who's affected." She got on a plane to San Francisco and sat down with Leon with the Control Bull's-Eye tool in hand.

Leon was willing to talk things out. He admitted that he just wanted to get the problem under control. It worked out better when he thought about Lily's question, which was "What, in fact, do we need to control?" It turned out they both wanted a situation in which Dad had maximum mobility, but there was no extra physical burden on Mom.

Lily and Leon could influence whether Mom and Dad moved out of their home, but in the end that was their parents' decision.

What they couldn't control was their anxiety over the failing health of both their parents. It was simply a sad but true part of life. Lily helped Leon express grief over this and his exasperation that he couldn't really help his father regain the health he'd had in middle age.

New Beginning

Lily's first instinct was that she'd have to quit her job and go to Hawaii and care for her parents as a part of her filial duty. This time the typical feminine reaction wasn't practical. "Wait a minute," she said. "I've got a family here that needs me."

Instead she did research on the benefits her company offered. One was assistance in caring for elderly parents. It put her in touch with the elder assistance available where her parents lived. One benefit was a home nursing service that would send a trained nurse to the home every afternoon for several hours. Furthermore, there was no cost for this service.

When she told Leon he said, "Maybe this could be the start of a solution that would let our parents stay in their home. I need to check out if the insurance could cover nursing care for the mornings. We could also supplement with a private nurse if we had to."

Their parents loved the idea. It turned out they did have insurance coverage for the morning nurse. Between that and the city program, their dad got the care he needed.

Change Lessons from Lily and Leon

1. Take time to grieve for what was past (Change Step 1, *Say Goodbye*).
2. Search for ways to take control during change that are beneficial to all parties (Brock Change Skill 4, *Flexibility*).
3. Think beyond the stereotypical response to change to a response that is beneficial to all parties (Brock Change Skill 2, *Reframing*).
4. Spot the specific places where you can be in control during change. This can make you feel better, as it did for Lily and Leon in identifying the things that were totally out of their control (Change Step 2, *Middles*).

Remembering Our Differences

Men and women are different in the ways they approach change. These differences come out under the stress of having children and caring for elderly parents. Men at first resist and then like to take action. Women don't understand this male approach to change. They like to plan, research, and visualize what the new place is going to be like.

When men and women understand how they each approach change, their natural strengths can be used to make parenting an easier, and even enlightening, experience. By understanding how the other gender approaches the three steps of change, they can help each other in the three change steps of *Say Goodbye, Move Through the Middles,* and *New Beginnings.*

When making a move, each of us needs to sharpen our ability in the five Brock change skills: *Personal Vision, Reframing, Emotional Resilience, Flexibility,* and *Self-Sense.*

Jose and Valerie were able to enjoy their new baby even more because they came to understand each other's change style and to strengthen their capacities for managing change. Sheila has learned to use her feminine strengths in coping with change and showing her daughters how dreams can be accomplished. Lily and Leon have come closer as they each contributed their change management skills in handling their father's stroke.

PART IV

Changes in Location, Health, and Finances

This section describes how women and men approach things in different ways when change occurs in their everyday lives.

In Chapter 12, we show how men and women react differently to the challenge of a move. Chapter 13 describes how to live with your partner more successfully during sickness and health. In Chapter 14, we'll see how men and women approach finances and changing financial health.

Chapter 12

The Challenge of a Move, Across the Street or Across the World

AMERICANS HAVE ONE OF THE MOST MOBILE CULTURES IN THE world. On average, we move once every seven years. A change in where we live is important on so many levels. Many of us experience the challenges of moving to a new place early in our adult lives at the same time we are also experiencing new relationships with the opposite sex, marriage, schooling, or a new job.

Women react very strongly to moving. So do men, but in different ways. Knowing how as women or men we react differently to change can make it easier. Take Max. He was able to create a life for himself in Paris when his wife's job mandated a move. He used the Brock Method to improve his change skills and understand how his wife, Lynn, was coping with the change.

Jane, a successful real estate executive, told us, "While I'm not certain gender is the controlling factor in how one manages changes, I have observed that men seem far more resistant than women in making change. I think men generally prefer to remain in unhappy relationships, for example, and 'make the best of it' (perhaps finding gratification elsewhere), rather than seeking counseling or divorce. I think they stay with less-than-satisfying employment longer than women. Our culture tells them to be manly, to 'suck it up, don't whine,' and 'that's life.' I see it particularly when they're asked to move, either to a new community or to downscale."

Max certainly typified that type of man, who wanted to stay where he was planted—in Max's case, Atlanta. He was a corporate lawyer, not too happy or successful in his job. The one bright spot in his daily life was getting home to the lovely house he and Lynn had built in the suburbs.

The Research: What She Said; What He Said

Lynn was ecstatic when she got the news of her transfer to Paris. "Fabulous," she said, "It's a great assignment and this will get Max out of his horrible job situation. Just imagine how exciting it'll be to have an apartment on the Champs-Élysées." As a woman she was already visualizing what their family life in Paris would be like.

Imagine her confusion when Max was cool to the news and reluctant even to consider the move. Our data suggest that it's harder for a man with his left-brained, action-oriented tendencies to visualize a new situation. He didn't want to complain, but he felt threatened and certainly didn't want to leave their lovely home.

Women find it easier to visualize a positive outcome to change than men.

Fortunately, Lynn and Max had a good marriage. She didn't become upset or angry with him, realizing that as a man, he might resist the change more and needed to work through it in his own way.

Lynn had bought our previous book as a forty-third birthday present for Max. He remembered that he liked the structured approach to change and decided to dig it out. His first impulse was just to say "No." But because he loved Lynn and wanted to support her, he decided he'd try to reserve judgment on the move and rethink his initial reservations.

Reframing

Max started with Brock Change Skill 2, *Reframing*. It just popped out to him as he flipped through the book. "What other ways could I see this move, besides a way to tear me away from a home I love," Max questioned (and also admitted), "and away from a job I really don't like?" He listened to himself and became his own reframing buddy.

Max continued his discussion with himself. "I've been thinking that I want to put more balance in my life. I need to work and am a trained lawyer, but maybe there's a different way to use those skills." He decided to have a talk with the alumni outplacement office of his law school. "What," he asked, "do you have in Paris for an American-trained lawyer with sixteen years of corporate experience?"

Max, who had begun his thought process with just one of the five Brock change skills, now started to use all five. Reframing was the beginning, and it allowed him to have the breakthrough idea. He expressed his need for increased emotional resilience by addressing his need for a less stressful, more agreeable job. Flexibility practice came out as he separated his job search into first finding leads, then interviews.

Remember the five change skills of the Brock Method:

1. Create a personal vision.
2. Reframe.
3. Build emotional resilience.

4. Practice your flexibility.
5. Increase your self-sense.

Max defined his personal vision as finding a job in Paris that used his training and experience. As he worked through that part of the exercise, he added the desire to hold on to the house in Atlanta that they both loved. As he told Lynn of his plan, she quickly jumped on the bandwagon because Max was getting excited about making the lifestyle change work for both of them. They decided they would rent out the house in Atlanta while they were in Paris.

Now, two years later, Lynn has completed her assignment in Paris. Max is reluctant to move because he has enjoyed their tenure in Paris so much. The job he got as legal counsel to the French-American Chamber of Commerce expanded his career choices immensely. And he loved helping French companies learn about U.S. law in order to enable them to establish branch offices in the United States.

Max is thinking about setting up a consultant's practice from his home in Atlanta, from which he will help European companies work through the maze of U.S. laws in order to be able to establish themselves in this country. That would also enable him and Lynn to travel back to Paris to show off their new twins.

Change Lessons from Max and Lynn

1. Allow your partner to react to changes in his or her own way (Brock Change Skill 4, *Flexibility*).
2. Use the five Brock change skills in whatever order helps you the most (Brock Change Skill 4, *Flexibility*).
3. Happy outcomes usually drop in from unexpected sources (Brock Change Skill 4, *Flexibility*).

Another Approach to Change of Location

It has been a different story for Richard and his wife, Stacie, and their family. Richard has had to move his family many times as he progressed along the promotion track in his company. In order to ease the stress of uprooting the family and finding a new home, he always has Stacie accompany him on the get-acquainted interview. Her job was to locate comfortable living accommodations, even if they were just going to be temporary.

It's ironic that Stacie doesn't have a traditional job because Richard is such a supporter of women moving up through his large, traditional company. She's a commercial artist and has been able to find work as they've moved to keep up with Richard's fast-changing career. She's also been able to create a nurturing home for him and their son, Chuck.

Say Goodbye

Richard never really says goodbye to the past to the extent that the rest of his family does. As he's moved upward through the company, he has kept the same group of colleagues and he is well known within the company. No matter what location he's in, the company is pretty much the same, so he just applies his skills as he has always done. This fits well into the male style of never having to take Change Step 1, *Say Goodbye*.

On the other hand, as a woman, Stacie is responsible for recreating the home in pretty much the same way no matter where they are. She has used her feminine change style to create rituals of saying goodbye whenever a move is called for. She always holds a party for Chuck to say goodbye to his friends when his father's job transfers the family to a new location, and they've built a tradition of collecting e-mail addresses so that Chuck can keep up with the friends he's made in that town.

Move Through the Middles

To get through the Middles fast, Stacie always goes with Richard to the first interview in the new location. She has a network of realtors across the country and a description of the house she wants. It's always a four-bedroom split colonial in a neighborhood with a good Catholic school for their son, Chuck, and no more than an hour's commute for Richard.

She has the rooms painted in exactly the same colors so her furniture looks right. Richard stays in a hotel until the house is ready, and then Stacie and Chuck join him at a break in Chuck's school schedule.

This seems artificial to most of us, but it's Stacie's transition plan that works for every move. She takes comfort that it's pretty much the same every time. It takes the sting out of the challenge of moving and lets her concentrate on exploring and settling in to the new location.

New Beginnings

Once the furniture arrives and the pictures are up, Stacie has a fondue party for Richard's colleagues and their spouses. She also encourages Chuck to pick out friends who can come to his next birthday party.

They've had a tradition about starting a scrapbook about each new location. She keeps in touch by sending out Christmas letters, cleverly describing what's unique about the place where they live.

This is Stacie's approach to the challenge of moving that's been so much a part of her life. Because she's overcome her feminine hesitation to move through the Middles fast with a process that always works, she is able to put a lot of effort into making a new beginning that's positive for the whole family.

She uses her feminine change skill strength of making a picture of the new start that helps everyone. Actually, because

Stacie is an artist, these pictures are extremely good and have been featured in Richard's company's employee newsletter.

Change Lessons from Richard and Stacie

1. Develop a process for getting through the Middles fast (Change Step 2, *Middles*).
2. Respect each person's change style, as Stacie does in insulating Richard from changes at home (Brock Change Skill 2, *Reframing*).
3. Create rituals for saying goodbye (Change Step 1, *Say Goodbye*).

When Change Moves to Your Neighborhood

In another part of the country, we find that change challenges can come when your neighborhood becomes a different place to live. In Philadelphia, the Pearsons had always lived in the pleasant roughhouse in a stable blue-collar environment. Over the years, this area of Philadelphia had welcomed waves of new immigrants as they started their path of upward mobility. The Pearsons had been newcomers once too, but they felt threatened when the Singhs moved in next door.

> Men and women react to change on different time schedules.

Creating a Personal Vision

"That's it," said Ralph Pearson, "Those new people are ruining the neighborhood, putting up a shrine in their back yard. Not even to mention those weird smells at dinnertime. If I'd wanted to move to Calcutta, I'd have done it." Ralph didn't like the way the neighborhood where he'd grown up was changing.

His wife, Natalie, loved her husband, but she knew he didn't see anything positive about the wave of new immigrants from India that were influencing his neighborhood. How could she get him to see it in a different light? She remembered how Ralph had loved his days in the U.S. Navy, when he truly got to see the world. He had returned from one trip with a beautiful length of sari silk from India, which she'd had made into a party dress and with the leftovers created pillow covers for their living room sofa.

She decided that she would get Ralph to start talking about the experience of buying the silk and what that country was like. It was easy to get him started reminiscing. "The smells," he said, "I'll never forget the way India smelled; it was truly foreign and exciting."

The delicate part of the maneuver came in now. "Ralph," she said, "you'd always wanted to go back and take me there." She waited for a positive reaction, which she got. "Those people next door come from there; maybe Mrs. Singh would teach me how to make a curry."

Reframing

"Okay," Ralph smiled, "I know what you're doing, but I guess I've been a little intolerant of our neighbors. Make the curry and maybe it would even be good to invite them over for an old-fashioned Irish stew."

Natalie's effort to create a different vision of the new neighbors allowed Ralph to reframe what their differences could mean to the Pearsons.

Emotional Resilience

The Singhs did come for dinner. Ralph had a good time and said he'd not laughed that much in a long time. They even liked his navy stories.

The Singhs shared their insight that laughter was very much a part of the tool they were using in the struggles they were using to adapt to their new country. "It takes real emotional resilience to be an immigrant," said Mr. Singh. "In our hometown we had a Laughter Club and every week we'd go to a half-hour routine where we just laughed. There were all kinds of different ways to laugh. There's the lion laugh, the arguing laugh, the chuckle, the groan. I was always amazed how much better I felt after those sessions."

Ralph wasn't sure he was quite ready to join a Laughter Club, but he did admit to enjoying watching the reruns of *Gilligan's Island* on cable.

Change Lessons from Ralph and Natalie Pearson

1. Use humor to help others develop their change skills (Brock Change Skill 3, *Emotional Resilience*).
2. Irritation is often a sign of inflexibility. Take it as a sign to check out whether you're using your Brock change skills (Brock Change Skill 4, *Flexibility*).
3. Men and women react to change on different time schedules (Brock Change Skill 2, *Reframing*).

The Change Challenges of Retirement

Louise used a surprising approach to change when she relocated to a retirement community. At eighty, she knew she wasn't going to be able to live alone in her comfortable home much longer. She had talked it over with her son, who lived in New York City, and they both agreed that it was time to shop for a new living arrangement.

Finding the place wasn't too hard. She had many friends in the community. When one of them moved into a nearby retirement community, she decided she'd buy in, too. She told them she would move in September, nine months away, when a new wing of the development opened. That gave her some time to prepare for the change.

Now the question was how to say goodbye to her old life and transition into the new. She looked at how she'd lived in the twenty years since her husband had died and her son had left home.

Emotional Resilience and Flexibility

Louise realized she'd become more than a little inflexible. She liked to watch "her" television shows and usually ate in front of the television. Because her eyesight was reducing her ability to get out, she had started to go only to the events she was accustomed to, like church on Sunday mornings, bridge on Tuesday nights, and grocery shopping on Wednesdays when the specials came out. She decided she needed a "tune-up" before she started her new life.

First of all, she decided she'd take some active steps to make her mental and physical health as good as she could make it. All those evenings of eating in front on the television had put some weight on. She called her local senior's center and signed up for a weight reduction and exercise program. She then took the big step of arranging to get cataract surgery. It wasn't easy, and it took a while to recover. But she was glad she had done it, even if it did mean she could now see her wrinkles and white hair more clearly.

She decided she was going to take on some new projects that she could carry through to her new home. She had the advantage of being in the same community.

One thing she started was a writing class for older people to make a record of their lives and the times in which they lived. Another was getting friendly with computers. She bought an inexpensive one and started corresponding with her son via e-mail. She figured that even if she couldn't drive as much now, she could still let her fingers do the driving.

Sense of Self

Louise had grown up in a time when assertiveness wasn't a quality women cultivated. She started reading up on how to get what you want. She practiced her negotiation skills with the developer in the senior center. Since her unit was in a new building, she was able to specify many of the details. For example, she wanted a blue bathtub, commode, and sink to match her favorite blue towels.

This is an extraordinarily good plan for someone relocating to a senior center. A common problem at such a place is not feeling at home. By bringing some favorite possessions— a picture, a rug, a chair—Louise made her new home feel less institutional.

Personal Vision

Louise looked around her and decided on the parts of her home that she really loved. What could she take with her? She loved her sunny kitchen window and the sill where she fed the birds. Her bathroom was old, but it had an especially roomy bathtub.

She went to the contractors with these two desires. They were accommodating in helping her select a unit where the kitchen would get a lot of sun. They even agreed to put hooks for birdhouses outside the kitchen window. For the large-size tub, they told her she'd have to pay extra. But she agreed, knowing she really loved the luxury of a long bath.

Louise has taken the move very well. She says that, if anything, her life is now more exciting than it was. The writing class has taken off, and she's nearly completed her biography, which she plans to give to her son on his next birthday.

Change Lessons from Louise
1. It takes time to handle major changes. Be patient with yourself (Brock Change Skill 3, *Emotional Resilience*).
2. It's never too late to improve your physical state (Brock Change Skill 4, *Flexibility*).
3. Take on new interests at every stage of your life (Brock Change Skill 4, *Flexibility*).

Remembering Our Differences

Our studies consistently show that men and women are different in the ways we approach change. The stress of moving is one of the most obvious ways in which each gender has entirely different coping mechanisms. Men at first resist and then like to take action. Women don't understand that approach. They like to plan, research, and visualize what the new place is going to be like.

When men and women understand how we each approach change, the natural strengths can be used to make moving an easier and even enlightening experience. By understanding how the other gender approaches the three steps of change, we can help each other as we make progress through the change steps *Say Goodbye, Move Through the Middles,* and *New Beginnings.*

When making a move, we need to sharpen our abilities in the five Brock change skills, which means creating a *Personal Vision*, figuring out how to go about *Reframing*, increasing our *Emotional Resilience*, developing *Flexibility*, and creating a stronger *Self-Sense.*

Max was able to create a whole new—and happier—working life for himself by reframing what he had initially seen as the problem of his wife's reassignment to Paris. We learned from Stacie that the feminine skill of creating rituals

Twelve Ways to Help a Man Move

1. Most men like structure, so help him create an action plan for the move.

2. Give him space to act immediately on getting to the new location.

3. Help him connect new situations with positive experiences in his past.

4. Stimulate laughter whenever possible.

5. Don't expect him to be able to listen much about your worries during the move.

6. Get him to say goodbye before going on to the next step.

7. Bring along some positive tokens of your previous life.

8. Expect that he may be assertive with the people hired to help you. Don't take it personally.

9. Encourage his natural tendency to move through the middle step of change fast.

10. Don't expect him to talk to his friends or family much about the change.

11. Focus him on tangible decisions.

12. Make him feel like he's in control of the move.

Twelve Ways to Help a Woman Move

1. Women take time to say goodbye, so give her advance warning.

2. Encourage her to tell you what she absolutely needs in the new location.

3. Encourage her to be specific about what would improve her life in the location.

4. Stimulate laughter whenever possible.

5. Be especially careful to show her you're listening during the move.

6. Give her control over as many decisions as she's comfortable with.

7. Bring along some positive tokens of your previous life.

8. Identify the relationships you want to continue in your new location and decide how to do it.

9. Create a process to get through the middle step of moving even though it might be uncomfortable.

10. Use friends and family to give you support during the changes of moving.

11. Remember to compliment your partner for her successful management of the moving process.

12. Create a common vision of the good the move can bring.

to say goodbye can help the whole family. We saw how Valerie's good humor helped Ralph increase his flexibility skill in adapting to an irritating new neighbor. And Louise can teach us all how to reinvigorate our self-sense at any age.

There are many ways that a woman can help a man to cope with the change of a move. A woman can be most helpful in a relationship by leading a man to the natural strengths that women seem to have in times of change. Some examples of these are being flexible, talking about fears, and reaching out to others for help. It's easy for many women to overlook their important contribution to coping with change.

Most men feel comfortable controlling a move to a new location in a direct manner. They concentrate on tangible, problem-solving things: How much does the move cost? What is the best timing? How much does it cost to buy another house? When will the new job start? How can we get two cars to one distant city? As we have seen in our book's title, men tend to believe that there is a rational, practical way to get from one place to another—just follow the directions on a map—while women look for guideposts along the way and seek advice on how to get where they are going.

No doubt, the focus on the practical that comes naturally to men is an essential part of a person's ability to successfully move themselves and all their possessions. But men frequently don't consider how to successfully move a relationship to a new home. That's where women come in. They are natural nesters, and they instinctively focus their energies into doing things for their partners.

The need to nurture a personal relationship at a time of moving is not a natural thing for a man to consider. Women, knowing this, can contribute much to strengthening the relationship by helping in little ways to smooth the transition.

Chapter 13

The Change Challenges of Health Throughout Your Life

CHANGES IN YOUR HEALTH OR THE HEALTH OF ANYONE IN YOUR family can cause you to make alterations in lifestyle. With health, the female strategy is to do research and make contacts. With a serious illness, women will consult more than one doctor, become an expert on their disease, and be more open to experimental treatment. Men are more likely to work through it without articulating their needs.

Peter, a typical New York City business owner in the garment district, had always believed that if he ate right, exercised, slept enough, and minimized his bad habits, he'd be healthy. An unexpected diagnosis of diabetes changed his whole world.

John, a divorcé, was raising his two teenage boys when he was struck by a minor heart attack. It changed his life—as he would tell you, for the better.

Janet reveals what she learned about managing change when she found out she had breast cancer.

The Research: What She Said; What He Said

Peter was astonished when, during a routine physical exam, his doctor gave him a diagnosis of diabetes. Peter worked long hard hours, and his wife, Isabella, had insisted he have a checkup for his fortieth birthday.

Facing a profound change in Peter's health and their lifestyle, they applied that same energy to creating a new lifestyle to incorporate the treatment for Peter's disease. Isabella was a former ballet dancer who now taught classes at a local studio. When she got the news, she was saddened. "What do we see our lives becoming?" she asked, starting the process for creating a personal vision.

Creating a Personal Vision

Isabella insisted on going to a specialist with Peter to hear exactly what modifications he would need to make in order to live with his diabetes. In this way, she was following her feminine style of coping with change in getting as much information as possible. Peter wouldn't have made such a big case of it, but he knew it was important to her.

After a visit to the specialist, during which he found that he now had more options, he also made a mental note to listen more.

Peter and Isabella used the Mix 'n' Match Tool to sort through their options. In the first column, what they had going for them was the healthy lifestyle of a good diet and a regular exercise program. Only minor modifications were required for the diabetic requirements. Peter's dedication to his job was a real passion. With the hours he put in every week, both thought this was the place where some new approaches should be considered.

Peter, his sister, and brother had inherited the business and made it a point of pride to satisfy every demanding customer. However, every year the garment business was growing more difficult, and much of the business was moving out of the country.

Reframing

The question for Peter and Isabella became how Peter could fulfill his obligation to his family business (his passion) using his skill and training in finance (his strength) but work fewer hours (a big need). Once the question was framed so specifically, Peter went to his brother and sister. He was reluctant to ask for help. He'd always been the strong older brother who knew all the answers.

He told them his medical diagnosis and asked for their ideas. His sister suggested that her oldest son come into the firm, as he wanted to do. He had been working several years in the tax and accounting department of a large firm in the city after getting his MBA in finance. "You could remain the chief financial officer, but Marty could pick up most of the day-to-day financial management and travel," she suggested.

Both Peter and Isabella were delighted with the arrangement and set about deciding how to use the extra hours.

Emotional Resilience

While she was searching the Web for ways to manage disease, Isabella found studies that showed the positive effect of attitude on disease.

She and Peter decided they'd take on the challenge of inserting an hour of laughter into their lives every day. They were amazed at how hard it was. They ended up being trained as clowns. Now they volunteer at a local hospital and put on shows for sick children.

When you become a clown, you pick a personality. Both were surprised that Peter picked a sad clown personality. It helps him express some of his frustration at having diabetes as a part of his life.

Isabella also brought the concept of recovery time from her experiences as a ballerina. "After every performance, I'd have to spend an hour with a massage therapist," she told Peter. He heard the message in what she was saying. It's not practical for him to have a massage every day, but he does have one at the end of every workweek.

Change Lessons from Peter and Isabella
1. When big changes happen, take time to formulate the question of exactly what it is that you want (Change Step 1, *Say Goodbye*).
2. Ask for help (Brock Change Skill 3, *Emotional Resilience*).
3. Listen (Brock Change Skill 2, *Reframing*).
4. Positive attitude is effective medicine (Brock Change Skill 3, *Emotional Resilience*).

The Male Perspective

John was a dedicated corporate executive at a food distribution company, working long hours and traveling extensively. He'd been divorced five years and had joint custody of his two sons, Michael (sixteen) and Ken (ten).

One autumn morning he woke up and didn't feel right. Pains in his chest and left arm turned out to mean exactly what he feared: heart attack. At the emergency room, the doctor told him he'd done the right thing. The damage was minimal, but he would need to change his life. He had to reduce his work and travel schedule. He would also need to change his diet, exercise regularly, and go on a medical regime to lower his cholesterol and blood pressure.

His first reaction was the typical male one: "Oh no, I could never make that kind of change. I'll be okay anyway."

Saying Goodbye to the Past

What John was experiencing was the typical reaction to the first step of change. He couldn't believe what had just happened (even though the tubes running out of his body should have helped). His risk tolerance was out of whack. He thought he was going to be able to continue living his life the same as he always had.

It's easier for a man to experience major denial when he has to say goodbye to a part of his life. In this case, it was a matter of life and death for John to change his lifestyle. As John was an intelligent man, the necessity did sink in gradually, and he got through the embarrassment of grieving over the emotional losses.

He became closer to his sons. His father had died when John was thirteen. John decided he needed to see his boys more than just on weekends; he needed to become an important part of their lives. He decided to reach out, talk with them, express his desires, and trust that they would respond. They did.

During change, reach out, communicate more, and express trust.

What he realized when he talked with his employer was that he was not going to be able to continue to do his old job. Fortunately, the company was going through downsizing and was happy to offer him a generous severance package. By law, they had to continue his medical benefits for eighteen months. Any law allowing twice that time will be welcome news.

It was a hard thing to do, but John decided to take the impact of the second big life change—quitting his job—and manage both the change in his health and in his job together. When the number of changes is increased, stress is not just added to but multiplied.

Get Through the Middles Fast

What John needed was a way to get through this period fast. He had the structure of the severance income and medical benefits, but he needed to rethink his life. His brush with death had made him consider what was important in his life. John came to two conclusions: living it well, and seeing to it that his two sons got every advantage he could give them.

John now had time to consider whether the portion of his life he had been spending on work (80 percent) was in line with what he wanted. However, he also needed to get through this period of convalescence and get over the loss of ego-satisfaction his old job had given him. He'd seen men his age drop out of work and go completely to pieces.

John decided to take some calculated risks.

Take calculated risks to get through the Middles fast.

He took advantage of the male talent to take quick, direct action. What he did was ask his employer if they would hire him as a part-time consultant. He put together a proposal of specific projects he could work on and a budget for what it would cost the company. They realized they were getting a good deal economically, so they took him up on the offer.

With this, John had the temporary structure in place for the work part of his life. He then went about negotiating with his ex-wife to have the children live with him and visit with her on alternate weekends, reversing the pattern they'd had the last five years. He was surprised when she agreed with only minor modifications.

He was able to appeal to her desire to work full-time and the value she placed on the well-being of their sons. She'd had just finished her degree, which John had paid for. The boys were older and Michael was able to drive, so they were moving into a new life stage. She agreed they were at an age when they'd benefit from spending more time with their father.

Start a New Beginning

Now, what was John going to do with the rest of his life? He began by painting a picture of where he wanted his life to go. He started with the middle column of the Mix 'n' Match Tool.

First, he established that he wanted to have more time to spend with his sons. John also needed to re-educate himself regarding career options. He wanted to have a job that would allow him to provide for his sons and that would also let him be home to go to their school events, take Ken to his sports practices, and spend vacation time with the boys as a family. Second, John wanted time and space to be able to pursue painting. It was a passion he had had since he was a teenager and received his first set of oils.

Obviously, he had to find a way to make money where he would have control over his time. He'd always been intrigued with starting his own small business. He had very real skills built up as a marketing and sales expert for food distributors. He took another risk and approached a former workmate from the financial side of the business and asked him if he'd like to form a partnership. His former colleague agreed, and he and John went about the process of building a business plan and getting investors to put money into the new company.

John also made major changes to his home, which was once a New England barn. He created bedrooms and living spaces for his sons to reflect his new commitment to spending more time with them. The part of the home that gives him the most pleasure is the artist's studio, which gets north light. It's right by John's home office.

Another thing John did to make his new lifestyle work was to learn to cook by watching cooking shows on television. Among other inventive dishes, he now makes a healthy pizza that gets vegetables into everyone.

John made good use of the male approach to handling the steps of change. It's working for him. A woman would have gone about it differently, probably by seeking out more information and talking to more people. John's actions were specific and targeted. He now says that the day he had his heart attack was the happiest day of his life. It showed him what was truly important to his life.

Change Lessons from John
1. Overcome your natural desire to communicate and trust less during Change Step 1, *Say Goodbye*.
2. Take calculated risks to transitions through the Middles fast (Change Step 2, *Middles*).
3. Be specific about what you want from your life (Brock Change Skill 1, *Personal Vision*).

The Female Perspective

Janet had a similar health challenge to the one John had, but as a woman she approached it in a very different way. She and her husband, Bert, were on home leave in Florida from his assignment in Russia. They'd both always loved the exotic, and the time they were spending in Moscow was a dream come true.

They were shopping at the local mall when Janet saw a breast cancer prevention group's van parked in the lot. The group was offering free mammograms. Never having had one, she said, "Why not? It'll just take a few minutes."

She returned to the car an hour later in a state of shock. "They want me to go to the hospital as soon as possible for a biopsy," she said. "They think I have early-stage breast cancer."

It turned out that the screeners were right. She did have cancer, even though she'd had no symptoms. She felt that she was the poster child for preventive screening. Now, Janet had to rethink how she was going to spend the next year of her life.

In the way women commonly handle change, she immediately started talking with other people who'd had this stage and type of cancer. She researched the best places to get treatment and the type of treatment choice to make.

Saying Goodbye to the Past

The first thing Janet needed to say goodbye to was a return with Bert to Russia for the next year. He would stay in Florida until she had the partial mastectomy surgery and breast reconstruction, but then he'd have to get back to his job.

She was going full-steam ahead communicating with every one of their friends and Bert's colleagues, until Bert finally had to tell her he was getting uncomfortable. "I know it helps you to talk about it, but I need to just have some time when we aren't discussing your disease. I'm fully behind you in treating this thing, but let's just decide something and do it." Initially, her feelings were hurt, but then she realized he was handling the change in the way that was natural for him as a man.

Move Through the Middles Fast

Janet did everything she could to continue to share the experience with him. She was very clear with him that she needed his support. They installed a modem for high-speed Internet access so they could communicate every day by e-mail.

With her doctor's approval, Janet set a goal. If everything was proceeding normally six months after the surgery, she would then rejoin Bert in Moscow.

Meanwhile, rather than dwell on anxiety about the surgery, she created a medical and psychological recovery plan.

Start a New Beginning

The surgery went well, but Janet decided to be doubly safe and followed up with chemotherapy.

Her physical therapist helped her design a program of moderate exercise and good diet. She started gardening and at last got the hibiscus growing off her front porch and the herb garden started in the back.

She decided she needed some unconditional love and approval in her life, so she went to the animal shelter and picked out Shadow, a two-year-old black cat with white paws.

Besides her frequent e-mails to Bert, Janet also kept up her Russian language lessons. In six months, she and Shadow were ready to get on the plane to Moscow with their Russian visas.

Change Lessons from Janet

1. Remember that your partner is not likely to handle your change the way you do (Brock Change Skill 2, *Reframing*).

2. Don't take it personally (Brock Change Skill 5, *Self-Sense*).

3. Find out all you can about how to solve your change challenge, do it, and then let go of the anxiety (Brock Change Skill 4, *Flexibility*).

4. Concentrate on creating a nurturing environment during times of stress and change (Brock Change Skill 3, *Emotional Resilience*).
5. Create positive goals and timetables for achieving them (Brock Change Skill 1, *Personal Vision*).

Remembering Our Differences

Men and women can help each other during those inevitable changes in health if we remember how differently each gender approaches those changes. Men don't realize that their decisive approach confuses women. For women, it's easier to feel comfortable in the stressful situation of managing their health if their partners are willing to understand it's natural for them to cope with these changes in a very different way.

Women also need to understand that their approach to the stresses of a change in health—usually involving getting a group of friends together to talk—is not one that attracts men. It's better to define what you want, know what you have to give, and be assertive if you're seeking to talk with a number of men.

Both genders have a different approach to the three steps of reacting to changes in health. These methods work for them, but knowing how the opposite gender copes can make it work even better.

John took advantage of the masculine direct approach to work through Change Step 1, *Say Goodbye*. And he excelled in figuring out a successful strategy for him in Change Steps 2 and 3, *Move Through the Middles* and *New Beginnings*. His life is now much richer for the way he handled his heart attack. That's exactly the way Janet feels about her brush with breast cancer even though she coped with that health change in a more feminine way.

Peter and Isabella demonstrated how combining both the male and female approaches to building up their Brock change management skills brought them through a troubled time to think about it as a rich experience.

Chapter 14

Your Changing Financial Health

MEN AND WOMEN ARE DIFFERENT IN HOW THEY LOOK AT MONEY and financial security. Women need to understand that what might appear in a man as resistance to change may actually be the calm before the storm as he prepares to go into action. Men need to value the more analytic approach that women usually take, even though it can look like procrastination to them.

This chapter illustrates how men and women approach changing finances. Suzanne and Jack will tell you about the financial ups and downs of a career and growing family. We'll introduce you to Joy, a widow and retiree, and the way she lives.

You'll also meet Ellen. Ellen, a financial counselor, observes that men and women have a different reaction to changes in their financial picture, "Women are more mentally prepared and open to change. Men fear change inasmuch as it will force them to be more emotionally open and involved. Men can seem to resist and fight change. I see it in how they react to my recommendations for new investment strategies."

Ellen goes on to say, "When change happens suddenly, like a drop in the stock market, men seem to take it more in stride and act quickly. Men are more objective. Women tend to have an emotional attachment and can seem tied up in the details of the change. We see the path and plot to change, while men see the end of the path and 'just go for it.'"

The Research: What She Said; What He Said

Jack is a man of few words. He's bright and brave and has made an excellent career for himself in the software industry. One day early in his career, he was walking to his car in an executive office park. A thief, hiding in his backseat, forced him at gunpoint to go to the nearest ATM. "Withdraw all your cash," the man said. Thinking quickly, Jack reached for the card for a small inactive account they had and withdrew the total: $120.

His approach to financial management is the same. He gets the best job he can, no matter where it requires his family to live. The last move took them from Boise, Idaho, to California's Silicon Valley, which meant a large increase in salary but relocation into a very expensive area. When he was there on his job interview, he also signed a contract for the first house the realtor showed him.

Creating a Personal Vision

Jack doesn't think he needs to create a personal vision. He has one. It's to get the best job with the best opportunity for maximizing his salary to support his family.

Suzanne always needs to create a new personal vision for each location. She's done a great job in Boise of creating a nurturing home, even with the financial challenges of giving up her own high-paying job and having a baby.

With this latest move, she had new financial opportunities and challenges. When she looked at the first column of the Brock Mix 'n' Match Tool, Jack's high salary was an obvious strength, as were her professional qualifications. She had been in fundraising and was even able to find some part-time volunteer work at the Boise Art Museum to keep her resume up-to-date. Her daughter, Juliana, was now in school, so she had some more free time. She also had a network of alumni contacts from college.

The middle "Passions" column of the Mix 'n' Match Tool is long for Suzanne. At the top is her desire to create a nurturing home for herself and her family. But she also loves to work and get to know the new areas where she finds herself. The question after this California move was where in the Silicon Valley area she could find a match. But first, she had to sort out the challenge of finding the money to fund the purchase of the house that Jack had committed to.

Reframing

This required some reframing. Suzanne was irritated at first that Jack had jumped right in and committed to a house without consulting her. It was much smaller than the one they had in Boise and certainly lacking in any of the same charm.

When she expressed her frustration to Jack, he said, "Houses move so fast here and the market is so tight, I felt I had to jump at something that was at least suitable for us. I know you have sticker shock from the price, but it's a good buy for this market." This is certainly a good example of men's tendency for direct action.

Even with the maximum mortgage the bank would give them, there wasn't enough to make the down payment. Jack had pretty much thrown the problem in Suzanne's lap. Unfortunately, this is another masculine characteristic.

She talked with as many people as she could about how to find the money: the realtor, the human resources people at Jack's company, several of her friends, and her parents. The one extra asset they had was the company stock that Jack had received as part of his sign-on bonus. They borrowed against the value of the stock to make the down payment on their house. There was a little left over, so at least Suzanne could repaint the new home.

Emotional Resilience and Flexibility

Fortunately, Suzanne had been working on keeping her life in balance. In Boise, she'd worked to make a rich life, and even though she didn't have a paying work life, the volunteer work she did enhanced her professional qualifications as a fundraiser.

She structured a plan of attack for the saturated job market in the Silicon Valley. First, she took out a map of the area and created the circle of places where she could work and still get to her daughter's school for a 3 P.M. pickup. She was using the feminine approach to managing change by first collecting all the information she could.

Suzanne's equation also included the amount of money she needed to earn for them to keep up the payments on their house loans.

Jack was bemused at all her efforts, saying, "Why don't you just let me worry about how to meet the loan payments?" Suzanne listened and respected Jack for his love in wanting to protect her, but this only reinforced how she needed to work some things out for herself.

Sense of Self

Suzanne started studying how to present herself in the most credible way possible. To meet her financial goals, she had to get a high-paying job. Any organization in her area of Silicon Valley that needed to get contributions was on her list of targets. She embodied all the lessons of assertiveness in her presentation.

First, she made a thorough list of the strengths she could present at every interview she could possibly get. What exactly could she contribute to this company? She went so far as to do a little research on their markets and to outline what she could do for them to enhance their fundraising.

Next, Suzanne developed her own support network of new friends she'd found by attending alumni meetings of her college in the Silicon Valley. Some of them were able to give her leads to organizations that might be looking for a fundraiser.

It took fifty hours of Internet search, twenty-five hours of phone calls, and thirty-two interviews, but she finally landed a job that met her requirements.

Change Lessons from Jack and Suzanne

1. Reframe financial challenges as opportunities to find new sources of income (Brock Change Skill 2, *Reframing*).
2. Don't let your frustration at your partner's financial style interfere with the approaches that are successful for you (Brock Change Skill 3, *Emotional Resilience*).
3. Keeping your life in balance can provide a basis for moving volunteer efforts into a paying job (Brock Change Skill 4, *Flexibility*).
4. Acting fast is one financial strategy, and so is doing thorough research. They are complementary (Brock Change Skill 2, *Reframing*).

The Female Perspective

Joy was at a very different stage of life. An ebullient woman, she had a love of life that you'd expect from someone with her name. Her life had not been easy. Married to an alcoholic for many years, she had very little from Bill's life insurance when he died at fifty.

She went to work as a secretary at a government office, so when she retired, she had a small pension and social security. Her son, who is in delicate health, was really not able to give her any financial support.

When she retired, Joy made the unusual choice to stay in her small apartment in the Dupont Circle area of Washington, D.C. Most of her friends had decided to move south or into local retirement communities. Her apartment was rent controlled, and she liked her neighbors and the support staff in the building. Also, it was located on major bus routes.

Saying Goodbye

As she prepared herself for retired life, Joy made sure she took the important pieces from her fifteen years at her job with the federal government.

With a typical female approach, she took advantage of every opportunity for learning that retirement offered. There were lots of opportunities for training seminars, so she studied about everything she could, including courses on computers and the Internet, managing retirement on a small income, and our seminar on change. From that she learned to be active about planning rituals and ceremonies for saying goodbye. Besides a few symbolic pieces she took from her office, she asked to buy her computer so she could start her home office.

She was already thinking about what tools she had that could take her through the Middles fast.

Get Through the Middles Fast

Yes, Joy was going to use the Internet as a low-cost method of communication and entertainment while she settled into the retired life. Her colleagues and friends teased her a bit, saying she was a little old to become a computer nerd, but Joy proceeded anyway.

One of the bigger decisions she made as she went through the exercise on the Control Bull's-Eye was to cut out all the costs she could control. The big one was her car. She had needed it to get to the office, but frankly it was a big expense. And she'd faced the difficult fact that driving in Washington was hard even for a younger person.

When her workmates asked her what she wanted for her retirement gift, she turned away offers of watches and silver bowls and asked them to buy her a printer.

Start a New Beginning

Joy has jumped into her new life. One interest she's been able to explore is the game of bridge. She'd played with a group of women even since she moved to Washington fifteen years ago. Now she found she could find new partners and games on the Internet.

She has found a new goal for herself in life. Passionate about bridge, she decided she was going to take it on herself to make it a popular game among the new generation. What she has done is set up a Web site for bridge lovers, and she's getting hits from all around the world. This has brought in responses from people both young and old. Joy still hasn't explored all the ideas she has to bring the game to more young people, but she does know that following her passion has enriched her life.

Change Lessons from Joy

1. Open yourself up to learn new things at every age (Brock Change Skill 4, *Flexibility*).
2. Explore your passions without worrying about what others think (Brock Change Skill 1, *Personal Vision*).
3. When one stage of your life is over, say goodbye, and get on with what's next (Change Step 1, *Say Goodbye*).

Men, Women, and Money

Ellen manages investments for other people. She says men and women approach money with their own style.

"The biggest difference appears to be that women go more with their feelings," she observes. "Men are more analytical. Many times it is the woman in the family who really makes the financial decisions and more and more is the 'controller' of the investments. Men are more confrontational when things go wrong and are more apt to believe that the mistakes are some kind of personal weakness or someone else's fault like research, broker, etc. They also carry grudges."

On the personal side, Ellen is her own success story. She lives in a modest two-family home, renting out part to a large Asian family. They help her care for her new daughter, whom she recently adopted in southern China.

Remembering Our Differences

Men and women are different in the ways we approach change. The stress of a change in financial status is one of the most obvious ways in which each gender has entirely different coping mechanisms. Men at first resist and then like to take action. Women don't understand them. Women like to talk, do research, and then act. Men are apt to see this as pro-crastination.

We saw this with Suzanne and Jack and the way they both used the Brock change skills to support each other during a time of financial stress. Joy, as a retiree, showed us all how to grow in Brock Change Skill 4, *Flexibility*. And Ellen illustrated how our natural differences in gender influence our financial choices.

In the next several chapters, we'll illustrate the ways in which men's and women's differing approaches to change influence the workplace.

PART V

Change Challenges in the Workplace and the World

hapter 15 introduces a group of interesting people who have faced changes on their jobs and used their natural gender strengths to make changes work for them.

In Chapter 16, you see how men and women can work together when change comes to their lives in their own town, country, and even the world.

Chapter 17 deals with coping with the many changes that are happening to each of us all the time—even when we are often at different stages of change.

The book concludes with Chapter 18, which offers some insight on how to make change work for you.

Chapter 15

The Everyday Challenges of Change on the Job

THESE DAYS OUR JOBS ARE BEING DRAMATICALLY AFFECTED BY changes like new technology, layoffs, and the flattening of organizations into teams. In the twenty-first century, the most productive people may work from home, have several careers, and function more as entrepreneurs.

Women often have an easier time taking advantage of the more fluid workplace because they are less invested in the traditional work structure. Working women often have another life of family and friends outside the job. This frequently gives them an advantage over men when it comes to coping with life changes.

The workplace is a microcosm of the world. Every day, we face conflicts in our personal styles of facing change. This is a part of the diversity that is so much a challenge and a potential source of enrichment on the job today.

Finding yourself on a newly formed work team is very much a part of the job today. You might not even have known your teammates before. It's like that for Katherine.

She's a project manager for a large brokerage firm. The work force is extremely diverse, representing all races, lifestyles, and ages.

Katherine Skates Through the Middles

When Katherine was appointed as team leader for a group of five assigned to develop a name and package for a major new product for her division, everyone thought she was a good choice.

The vision for the team had been handed down from the president, so Katherine's job was to work her team through the Middles efficiently and effectively. Meanwhile, the whole organization was stressed from rapid growth. The employees were having trouble keeping their productivity up.

Katherine was disturbed that she'd been asked to take on yet another task. She felt that her work life was out of control. This is typical of Change Step 2, *Move Through the Middles*. Women are more vulnerable to feeling inadequate when they get new and challenging assignments. Privately, therefore, Katherine did her own Control Bull's-Eye to figure out where she could feel control.

First of all, Katherine reasoned, "I can control my own attitude about heading up this team. I'll think like a man; if they've got any insecurity about doing well, most men would just button it up and do it. Leaders have to act as if they know what they're doing. I've got to erase any sense of insecurity I have about getting the job done. If the president hadn't thought I was equal to the task he wouldn't have

> Women are more vulnerable to feeling inadequate with new and challenging assignments.

given it to me. A man would lead by example, so it's very important for me to exude confidence about the success of this project.

"But I'm going to get as much information as I can from the people who developed the product and those who have had this kind of assignment. And I'll use my professional associations and the Internet to get all the lessons I can about how to do this well."

Katherine immediately started talking with the people who had developed the product. As a woman, she had a natural tendency to be a good listener. And she went further; she asked others for support. She identified key members of her organization, like the sales force, who would have to get behind the decisions her team made. These people weren't in her control, but she could influence them. Here Katherine was exercising her natural approach to change as a woman by reaching out and finding out how others had done it successfully.

Also, as a woman she was sensitive to the social aspect of building a cohesive team. Everyone was in a different location, so most of the communication was going to have to be done electronically. Katherine started the process of getting the people on her team to know each other from a distance.

She met separately with each team member to find out exactly how much time he or she could spend on the project. That way she was able to take care of the personal "me" issues that anyone had.

The three men on the team thought it was a little silly that they had to submit short bios and pictures electronically. Unlike most men, Katherine listened to their concerns and then explained how she thought it would save time. As typical men, they were less sensitive to the social needs of a diverse group, but they were willing to give it a try. She went ahead but was careful to watch for adverse reactions. It turned out to be a good idea. That way when the team had their first face-to-face meeting, a lot of the social formalities were out of the way.

She had learned during the Middles that focus was essential and that in this first meeting she'd have to state her priorities clearly. As a woman, this wasn't her natural skill, but as a supervisor she'd learned to do it well. Katherine got the team to agree on a project plan and agree specifically what they would deliver and when. Each step was broken down into small pieces, with a completion date and a person responsible. Before the project plan was finalized, she examined it carefully, looking for steps that could be dropped as calculated risks and for those where there was a danger that the team had overpromised.

Katherine's Lessons for the Middles

1. Focus on what you can control. (Brock Change Skill 4, *Flexibility*).
2. Act as if you're succeeding (Brock Change Skill 5, *Self-Sense*).
3. Take care of the "me" issues in a hurry (Change Step 2, *Middles*).
4. Set short-range goals, and don't overpromise (Change Step 2, *Middles*).
5. Take small steps, and then be alert to the effect the change has on the situation. If you check in often, you have a chance to correct your course (Brock Change Skill 2, *Reframing*).
6. Take calculated risks (Change Step 2, *Middles*).
7. Skate fast. State priorities clearly, and focus on them (Brock Change Skill 1, *Personal Vision*).

Learning Flexibility

John's story is a classic. By putting flexibility into his life, and by adapting to change and altering his previously successful behavior, John opened the way to a new life of achievement. John was a young baseball prospect from a small farming town in Iowa. At nineteen, when he was still in his first year of college, he had a big fastball and a number of major league scouts interested in his every game. By the time John was twenty, he had signed up and was ready to enter professional baseball.

John's first three years in the learning curve of the minor leagues was a phenomenal time of success. John found that he could throw the ball harder than almost any other pitcher in the league. He always got more than his share of strikeouts and quickly became the star pitcher of any team he was on.

He rapidly progressed to higher levels and finally was asked to move up to the majors at the end of his fourth professional season. This was his big chance, the opening to fame and fortune that John had looked for during all of those years in the minors. He was brimming with confidence as he suited up in his new big-league uniform. After all, he thought, he was an up-and-coming star pitcher and a valued player for every team he had been associated with in the last four years.

John's first time out as a pitcher was a big success. He struck out the side during one inning and won the game handily. John was delighted, but his manager wanted to see if he could perform as well against a strong team. He went out again a week later and pitched against the Yankees. Again, his big fastball overpowered most of the tough Yankee lineup. As John was a big strong farm boy who could throw the ball nearly 100 miles an hour, even the Yankees had trouble hitting his pitches.

John was well accepted by his new major league team, and they invited him back for the next new season. He did well and became an important pitcher on the team's staff, contributing significantly to the team's first-place finish that year. So too, in the next two years, did John turn in an outstanding performance. But in his fourth year in the majors, John ran into a problem. Now the other teams were beginning to hit him regularly. He was not winning games. His career was beginning to tank.

During change, listen for adverse reactions and seek expert help.

A worried John sought out his pitching coach. "I don't know what's wrong, Coach," he said, "I'm doing the same thing that I do every year, but now they're getting to me. They always say, 'Do whatever got you here,' but it isn't working for me. What can I do?"

The coach, an old baseball man, immediately knew what the problem was. He had seen it many times before as strong young men came up and matured into seasoned players. Even the biggest and strongest pitchers reach the point where something comes off their fastball. They all get to the big leagues by pitching high and hard. The harder and faster their pitches, the more successful they are. Strength and speed are the keys to winning. Forget style, strategy, or skill. But sooner or later, age and the wear and tear on their arms catch up with them. They lose a little. Just a little off that fastball, and major league hitters jump all over it. When that happens, the end is near, unless they adapt and change.

The old coach said to John, "You must work on using other pitches to throw with your fastball. That way, the hitters won't know what to expect and that will slow them down. Right now, they know you are going to try to throw that fastball by them, and they are waiting to sit on it and swing for the fences. If you mix it up with another pitch, it will make your fastball more effective."

John thought about that advice for a while. Changing his pitching style in the middle of the season would be tough. Furthermore, there was always the danger of hurting his arm while he was experimenting with a new pitch and ending his career permanently. Besides, staying with what got him to the majors seemed to make a lot of sense. But he changed his mind on his next pitching outing.

John was called upon to open a three-game series in New York against the Yankees. His team was now contending for first place, partly because of his pitching efforts, and was looking to move up in the standings. Unfortunately, this wasn't to be the day for John's team. John was roundly clobbered by the Yankee hitters. Within three innings, he was in the showers wondering what had happened. He thought about the coach's advice, and he realized that the more experienced man had been right. Change has already arrived, and he must learn to adapt or lose his spot on the team.

John worked hard after that devastating experience to develop a good major league slider and curve ball. He worked with the pitching coach for several months until he was finally ready to try his newly developed pitching skills in a real game against (naturally) the Yankees.

Well, as you might imagine, since we are telling you John's story in a book about how to deal with change successfully, things went very well that day. John won the game against the Yankees and, moreover, did it with consummate skill and pitching expertise. He found that he didn't have to overpower the other team's batters. All he needed was the skill to throw a mixture of good pitches and the store of experience he had learned in his first four years in the majors. John went on to have a successful baseball career. Much to his delight, John found the key to managing change was practicing new ways to do things, and it resulted in a productive and successful career.

Change Lessons from John

1. Practice flexibility (Brock Change Skill 4, *Flexibility*).
2. Build from your strengths (Brock Change Skill 1, *Personal Vision*).
3. Ask for help (Change Skill 3, *Emotional Resilience*).
4. Listen (Brock Change Skill 2, *Reframing*).

Learning How to Say Goodbye

As a teacher, Rita has had to say goodbye to so many students that she now makes a little ritual out of it. She teaches kindergarten. Her students find it very hard to leave what's been a tight-knit group. She also gets very involved with each class and misses each one a lot over the summer.

So she's developed a way to give her something to remember each class. She makes a canvas of handprints for each graduating class and asks each student to sign his or her print.

Society is good about creating rituals for the big goodbyes like death, graduation, and retirement, but ours hasn't yet figured out what to do with changes like layoffs. Creating your own rituals to say goodbye helps clear the way to moving on to the next stage of change.

Create rituals for the small changes as well as the big ones.

Rita's husband, Phil, manages an advertising agency. He used some of her feminine skills in building rituals to cope with having to lay off staff during economic downturns. Rather than doing the large goodbye party and trying to make it a happy occasion, he makes it a more private affair. Having been in the situation himself, he knows it's hard to act happy when you're just mad at being laid off. In many ways men can cope with losing a job; it's easier for them than for women because their emotional side is more separate from their working side.

Because Rita and Phil talk about how they each approach change, through Rita's coaching Phil has become aware of how women react to being told goodbye by their employer. Though he originally developed his layoff conversation for his female employees, he finds it works well for men too.

First of all, he talks with each person and expresses his gratitude at the contributions made to his organization. This is sometimes not easy, as there is often anger and bitterness. He has a small token to offer, a golden apple, that symbolizes what he believes, that anyone who has worked for his firm becomes an alumnus.

It's been an amazingly successful program. In an industry as mobile as advertising, his is one of the few firms to have an active alumni group. Many of his former employees are positive about his agency, and some have even returned to work there. He, of course, welcomes them.

Rita and Phil's Lessons for Change Step 1, Say Goodbye

1. Acknowledge that saying goodbye is emotional (Brock Change Skill 2, *Reframing*).
2. If you initiate the goodbye, be sensitive to possible anger (Brock Change Skill 2, *Reframing*).
3. Create a symbol that helps remember the good parts of the old (Change Step 1, *Say Goodbye*).
4. Create rituals for small and large changes (Change Step 1, *Say Goodbye*).

Job Problems

Up until now we've been talking about personal relationships that involve two people with different views. A job involves many people, all with egos and different points of view. If you don't want disagreement, work alone. An organization thrives on many points of view, and the successful ones are able to listen and incorporate diversity into decisions.

Lorraine's firm was in the midst of being taken over by a European company. She found she welcomed the change the new bosses were bringing in. Her male colleagues wanted to hold to the old structure. How could she help them adapt? One way was to use her feminine tendency to research and reach out. She started e-mailing her counterparts in Europe to find out exactly how the management worked in their organization. She now has lots of examples of how the merger partner has succeeded in bringing in new litigation business. And they needed the help of Lorraine's firm to handle the extra workload.

Lorraine took a calculated risk during this major change and introduced a new framework for the organization. She developed an outline of the seven steps her firm could take to thrive during the merger. She helped her colleagues reframe. It wasn't easy, however; she had to go to one person at a time. But she started off doing it the smart way. She went first to the people who were more receptive and built up a critical mass of support with them.

Lorraine went on to excel at the law firm. She kept her feminine change skills but also decided she would take on excelling at competition, a tendency more characteristic of men. Sometimes you have to develop coping behaviors, even though it takes extra energy. She wanted to create a symbol to her coworkers that she was a champion. What she decided to do was sign up for the firm's basketball team. Even though she's only a little over five feet tall, she had such team spirit and athletic ability that she led the team to a championship.

Change Lessons from Lorraine

1. During change, communicate more often, even though your instinct may be to clam up (Change Step 1, *Say Goodbye*).
2. Teach others to reframe (Change Step 1, *Say Goodbye*).
3. Realize that changing minds is a multistep process. Start with those who are more receptive, and build up a critical mass (Change Step 2, *Middles*).
4. Sometimes change requires that you learn to excel in the opposite gender's style (Brock Change Skill 2, *Reframing*).

Using the Brock Change Method at the Start of a Career

Henry was working as a successful midlevel manager in a large accounting firm. In looking at what really stirred his passions—in other words, what made him really want to get out of bed on a cold rainy morning—he knew it was winter sports. He loves to ski, skate, and snowboard. How could he combine his accounting expertise and skill with his passion? He's now running the accounting department for a large ski resort in Colorado.

As a man, Henry had certain advantages over a fellow student, Sarah, in that women have less of a natural inclination to focus. However, as a woman, Sarah had some advantages of her own. She had come from her homeland of Israel to study for an MBA in Paris. An able student, she had excelled at a summer internship at Bankers Trust and was offered a job on their fast track. Tempted, Sarah decided to first think about what stirred her passions. She knew it in a second: it was her home country and her struggle to identify adequate water resources for a growing population in the new millennium.

Rather than just go back home and hope for the best, Sarah took advantage of being in Europe to learn all she could about how those countries had developed their water resources. She decided she would look for a job in the field she could hold for a few years and learn all she could about successful planning, funding, and executing of water conservation programs. Here she was exercising her natural feminine tendency to see what others were doing.

Change Lessons from Henry and Sarah
1. Don't live someone else's dream. Find your own (Brock Change Skill 1, *Personal Vision*).
2. Take calculated risks (Change Step 2, *Middles*).
3. Learn as much as you can (Brock Change Skill 2, *Reframing*).

The End of a Business Partnership

All things must end. This is true of countries, people, businesses, and relationships. It is also true of partnerships, particularly business partnerships. As in most things, men and women view this change through different eyes.

The Man's Approach to Change
Ramon had been in partnership with Dan for thirteen years. They had both started off in their medical equipment business after having spent many years in the corporate world. They had a lot in common. They both had a background in medicine. They both were family men. They both

wanted to be independent and work for themselves.

Right from the outset, they were successful. Over the years, their business grew and they both made a substantial living from it. In fact, they were both doing better than they ever had before. They soon discovered that they had very different personalities.

Ramon was very outgoing and a real leader. He felt comfortable taking charge in new situations and always had plenty of new ideas for building the business. Ramon always prepared and made presentations to new clients. He just seemed to know what people wanted and how to explain it to them.

Dan was much the opposite of Ramon. He was quiet and cautious. He never took the lead and frankly was happy to let Ramon be the front man. Dan was the one who always worried about the little things like overtime, employee procedures, and vacation schedules. Over the years, Dan became more and more reluctant to enter new business opportunities. He always said, "Let's stick to what we have. It's too risky to do anything new."

Ramon found himself getting more and more frustrated by Dan's conservative approach to business. Although at first Ramon didn't mind being the originator and the lead man in all of their dealings, after thirteen years he had grown tired of this arrangement. He found himself increasingly at odds with Dan over questions of how to service clients as well as their approaches to new business.

Men find it easier than women to discuss business problems frankly.

After thinking about this dilemma for over a year, Ramon had a frank discussion with Dan about their differences. Ramon came to the reluctant conclusion that he just could not feel comfortable doing it Dan's way. So, over the Christmas holidays, when things were the slowest, Ramon announced his retirement from the business. After all, he had enough money to live on, and he was still young enough to venture out on his own in some new enterprise.

So there it was. After sixteen years in the corporate world and thirteen years in business with Dan, Ramon was now completely on his own. He found that he loved it. For one thing, he realized that all the money that came into his new business was his own. He didn't have to divide it with his partners. Second, much to his delight, he could now make decisions on his own and not have someone else second-guessing him all the time. Happily, Ramon found that his judgment was almost always right on the mark.

As men reacting to the change stress of a growing business, Ramon and Dan reacted in the natural male way: If there's a problem, act to solve it.

It turned out that Ramon's decision to leave his partnership and go out on his own was a fortuitous move for his relationship with his wife, Gerry. She'd been involved in a business partnership for a decade, but as the business grew, her partner was becoming erratic and abusive. Gerry feared it was due to her increasing dependence on drugs to cope with the stress of a growing business.

As a woman, she had counseled Ramon to try to reframe his partnership woes, but in the end she wisely just let Ramon take the action he needed to in order to end it. She was wise in the ways men need to adapt to change. But now she needed to handle the change in her own business partnership.

The Woman's Approach to Change

Gerry had been a long-time consultant in partnership with a woman who was very dynamic and anxious for money and growth of the business. Gerry worked very hard to keep up with a heavy schedule of meeting clients and traveling to seminars and conferences. She made a very good living, but the strain had become fearsome over the years.

Ramon, Gerry's husband, had begun to notice a change in his longtime companion. This was truer than ever after Ramon had made his business change and had more time to be around the house and see Gerry during the day. Gerry worked at home on her paperwork, so she and Ramon had more face-time with each other.

Gerry's situation was becoming increasingly difficult. Like many women, she kept blaming herself for the problems in the partnership. Ramon was extremely helpful in showing her that her partner was putting unfair demands on her by asking that she continually be blamed for business problems.

One day, Gerry came home very upset. She told Ramon that her partner was just getting impossible, and they were on the verge of breaking up. Gerry was worried that she would not be able to carry on and make the kind of money that she had in the past without her partner.

Ramon remembered that he had the same feelings about himself when he left his longtime business partner. He encouraged Gerry to go her own way and make use of her own unique and valuable talents. After thinking about it for a time, Gerry finally decided to make a break with the past.

First of all, as a woman, she decided she'd take advantage of her natural skill in being emotionally resilient. The partnership stress had used up much of her reserve of serenity and self-confidence. She used the Brock Method to build on what came naturally, which in her case was Change Skill 2, *Emotional Resilience*. First, she took a look at the balance in her life and committed more of it to her own physical well-being. Gerry started really using her gym membership and even hired a personal trainer. After six months she was in the best shape she'd ever been in.

She enlisted Ramon's help in a laughter program. Always thought to be too serious, Gerry decided to keep a record of how many times she laughed on a typical day. It turned out she was lucky to get one chuckle in. Ramon was better at it, and as they started to spend more time together, she got up to five laughs a day.

While they were on a weeklong vacation, Gerry kept a record. They made it a game to see if they could get to a hundred laughs in a day. That meant

**Laughter is an impor-
tant tool during change.**

rules about what a laugh was. Would a smile count? How about a groan from a bad pun? They decided any vocalization counted. Even then, at 11:30 at night, they had to resort to reruns of *Seinfeld* to get their last two laughs to reach a hundred.

Gerry also devoted some time to thinking through her personal vision. What did she feel passionate about doing? She'd always been good at teaching. Her father had encouraged her to get an advanced degree, but she'd never had the time before. That was the thing she decided on, and it felt very fulfilling and a tribute to her father, who had died recently.

She now has a smaller but more interesting and less stressful consulting practice and is writing a book about her experiences. She has entered a Ph.D. program in education at a major university. Gerry realizes now that she has strengthened her marriage by making a change in a positive, systematic way and by working with her husband as a resource. Gerry now finds that she and Ramon are closer than they have ever been. This is because they worked through the change together and came through it with a better understanding of each other.

Change Lessons from Ramon and Gerry

1. Build on your own strengths, reacting to change as a man or a woman (Brock Change Skill 1, *Personal Vision*).
2. Use people who love you as a sounding board for business problems (Brock Change Skill 2, *Reframing*).
3. Focus on getting healthy during times of stress (Brock Change Skill 4, *Flexibility*).
4. Laugh more (Brock Change Skill 3, *Emotional Resilience*).
5. Changing times are a signal to look for ways to make your dreams happen (Brock Change Skill 1, *Personal Vision*).
6. Understand that most partnerships have a natural ending and let it happen. (Change Step 1, *Say Goodbye*).
7. Have the courage to break free. Much as we worry about bad things happening, it's the unexpected good things that most dramatically affect lives (Brock Change Skill 4, *Flexibility*).

Gender Differences in Job Loss

As we travel around the country and listen to people's stories of change, we find we always have more to learn. Again and again, we are struck by the stories we hear about people who have learned to protect and build their relationships by understanding how men and women face change.

With so many changes in our lives, and so many challenges to a stable and productive relationship with a spouse or lover, boss or employee, child or friend, it is vital to understand the human response to change. Although there are many factors at work in a change situation, coping and improving starts with understanding the differences between men and women.

Men and Job Loss

Carl lost his job after working at the same company for more than eleven years. He was a draftsman in an engineering department. A large conglomerate had acquired the company. Cuts had to be made. One Friday morning Carl was called into his supervisor's office and told that he need not report to work on Monday.

"It was something of a shock," Carl later said, "I knew that there were changes coming, but I never expected to be fired so soon after the acquisition." Carl went home and never returned to that plant again. Being naturally taciturn, the last thing Carl wanted to do was talk about it, to be reminded that "they don't need me anymore."

Carl's approach to his new situation was to tell his wife first. He knew she'd be wondering why he didn't go to work on Monday. Then he set out to find a new job by sending out his resume. He really didn't want anyone else to know that he had been laid off from his job. To him it was a sign of weakness. The fewer people who knew of his predicament, the better.

His wife, Elsa, had heard about how important it was to understand how men react to change differently than women. Elsa knew that apart from the financial strains of losing one of the household incomes, there was a real danger that the shock of being fired from his job would affect Carl's relationship with her.

Elsa took steps to make sure that she dealt with this change in her household in a productive way that would strengthen her marital relationship. First of all, she got clear in her own mind about not taking Carl's reaction to his job loss personally. Knowing him, and the way men typically go through a major change, she knew he was going to want to spend more time by himself. She reassured him that she loved him just as much as she did when he was working and would support him in any road that he took. She told him she'd be there to help when he was ready.

Carl didn't really want to discuss the details of losing his job, even to his wife. It was embarrassing. And besides, it wouldn't find him another job. His approach was to just keep moving forward. Elsa understood this oh-so-typical male approach. She knew that unlike women, men don't want or need to share their failures with others, particularly other men. Elsa knew enough about the dynamics of male/female change relationships that she refrained from pushing Carl to talk about it.

In fact, Elsa avoided the critical mistake that many women make in such circumstances. In an honest and loving effort to share the pain with their man, they force him to do what he is so very uncomfortable doing: talk about the problem. Since women are usually very comfortable reaching out to others, particularly women, and sharing their problems, many women assume incorrectly that men want to do that too. Our research indicates that usually nothing could be further from the truth. Attempting to force a husband or male friend to verbally relive or analyze a bad incident is usually counterproductive. If anything, it makes him feel more uncomfortable and drives him away.

Elsa knew that getting into an argument with her husband over his willingness to share feelings at this critical time would deeply hurt their relationship. Elsa avoided falling into a typical female mental trap, in which the man's lack of willingness to talk is equated to a lack of love for her. Instead, Elsa backed off and gave Carl his space while he burned up the phone wires and sent out resumes. Eventually he found another, higher paying position. Looking back on the episode, Carl now says of Elsa that "she really understood."

Women and Job Loss

Sure enough, Elsa lost her job about a year later. As a woman, she reacted very differently than Carl. She had been working at a bank in town for about three years. Elsa enjoyed the work routine of getting out each day and meeting people. The extra money didn't hurt either. But one day, as is so distressingly common in our society these days, Elsa's job was eliminated. When Elsa came home, she was in tears, even though she didn't feel as if she should be so upset.

Her first reaction was to pick up the phone and call her friend Anne. As it turns out, Anne had also worked at Elsa's bank briefly, so she at least knew some of the players. Anne had left to take a higher paying job in a doctor's office, and she knew the ropes of making a job change. The two women talked for hours that day about the bank, the boss, and the job. After they hung up, Elsa breathed a sigh of relief. She felt much better.

Later in the day Elsa talked to Carl about her job situation, and he was sympathetic. Carl helped Elsa because he made a conscious effort to listen rather than spout solutions. He helped just by being there for her. At this point Elsa didn't need a war plan for attacking the job market. She only needed love and understanding.

Carl knew from learning the Brock Method that women react to these things quite differently than he would. Remember that when he lost his job, he went on the attack, but he didn't share his true feelings with many people. However, he understood how Elsa would respond much better to the change in her situation if she were able to share her inner thoughts with her friends before taking direct action.

Carl correctly thought that his relationship with his wife, Elsa, would be much better served if he supported her quietly and let her deal with the situation in her own valuable but feminine way. Carl avoided prodding Elsa to action and let her own human reactions take charge. Because of this, the change made their relationship stronger rather than weaker.

Elsa now says of Carl, "He really understood."

Change Lessons from Carl and Elsa

1. Let other people go through change in the way that's best for them (Brock Change Skill 2, *Reframing*).
2. Reach out to assure the other person of your love and support (Change Step 2, *Middles*).
3. Don't take bad reactions to change personally (Brock Change Skill 5, *Self-Sense*).

Changing in Business as in a Garden

Gardeners know that each plant has a life cycle. At any given time, you may have one plant just starting to blossom and another ready to harvest. Being in business is like having a garden. In the beginning you plan and strategize; you have high hopes that your efforts will yield a bountiful harvest at the end of the season. Like a garden, which provides food, a business provides another of the necessities of life. Like a business, gardens go through changes before producing ripe fruit.

Finally, when all of the fruit is harvested, it is time to cut down the plants and let the soil renew. Perhaps, in the future, another harvest will be possible. Just as with gardens, one does not expect to pick ripe tomatoes in December.

The first thing you must do in any business effort is plant the seed. Usually that means you must have a plan, you must get people to work in your business, and you must have money to start. Just as in a garden, you must firmly plant the seeds of your business into fertile soil to have any chance at all of having a productive enterprise later. Weak ideas, like weak seeds, will not grow strong no matter how much care is given to them. And no business can grow into a strong one if it starts out in a hostile environment.

After the initial start of a business effort, it must be watered and tended to with great care until the seeds sprout into some form of visible enterprise. As the business effort grows, it demands more and more resources. During this time there are small growths, but they are mostly weeds, or at least weak plants that must be sacrificed in order to make room for the future producers.

In the next chapter you'll learn how to better understand the opposite sex's way of coping with external changes, whether they are major or minor.

Chapter 16

External Disruption and Changes

CHANGE HAPPENS TO ALL OF US EVERY DAY. EVERY LIFE HAS many disruptions and changes but hopefully very few major tragedies. The Greeks have a saying that the only way to avoid change is death. Our adaptability in the face of external changes has given the human species an advantage in evolution. One of the ways we survive during changing times is to have some redundancy built in to our society. If one person doesn't know the answer, then it's likely that someone else in the group will. Partnerships and teams are useful during times of change. Listening to both the female side and male side makes for better coping. Going it alone during change is difficult. That's what Rosa and Dick learned.

Facing Big Changes Together

Women tend to do more research and build up more slowly to a new start after an external tragedy. Men just *do* it. They may sometimes forget to voice their intent to start on Change Step 3, *New Beginnings,* until later. Many men are frustrated by what they see as women's procrastination. Men are simply more proactive. Yet it's often the case that the increased time women spend preparing for change allows them to come up with less traditional, more creative solutions. What are the male and the female approaches to *New Beginnings,* the third and final step of change?

As we remember from Chapter 6, Rosa and Dick had to manage a major disruption to their town's life. A big new casino was opening in their county. Most of the residents viewed it as a tragedy that would disrupt the serenity of their rural community. When we talked with them during our change research, Dick was the president of the city council and Rosa the vice president.

Dick's first response was to get the development to locate in a remote part of the county, so it would have little impact on town life. Not a bad idea, but Rosa suggested that it would be better to have the casino closer to their town and to work with the developers to see what services they would need from local merchants. This seemed illogical at first, because the casino intended to be totally self-sufficient, with its own restaurants, hotels, and shops.

"But," Rosa pointed out, "you'll still need services from our florist, gas stations, and medical facilities." Dick got on the bandwagon. He pointed out that not all casino visitors would want the relatively expensive hotel rooms, and they would look for less expensive motel rooms. Also, the casino would need to draw on the town's residents for its work force, as well as for housing for the employees who came from other places. By combining their two approaches, Dick and Rosa have been of much greater help to their community than either would have been alone.

Dick and Rosa were both sensitive to the need to get the word out about the new way to look at the casino. Dick left it up to Rosa to do most of the work of explaining the purpose behind the strategy and its desired outcome. As a woman, it made Rosa feel better to keep people in the know, and she was good at communicating. She organized a newsletter so that everyone in the town would know about the plans, and she published it weekly so that no one felt left out or surprised. It's a man's nature not to want to talk about an upcoming change until the solution is firmly in place. The irony here is that the act of communication itself is what strengthens us in our ability to face change together, by strengthening the invisible net that holds relationships together.

Dick agreed to work with Rosa as his co-leader, but he insisted on a plan. He said, "We need to clarify each person's part and get our marching orders straight." Dick went on to say, "It's been my experience that we must set out the steps for ourselves and the others involved in creating the new reality. Also, we have to be consistent and practice what we preach. We can't be one thing to our neighbors and another to the press. Thinking it out, talking about it, and writing it down helps to make it happen. I've learned from my business experience that new ideas are first only talk, and then a few incidences of the new behavior occur that you can celebrate. Then the new behaviors become a norm for the group."

Rosa agreed and added some ideas that were typical of the woman's approach. She suggested that they would need to build in some motivation here along with rewards for people who chose to take risks. "Let's find a way to celebrate small successes," she suggested. She developed an honor roll for the newsletter that recognized individual contributions.

Change Lessons from Rosa and Dick

1. Symbolize the new identity in a way that appeals both to men and women (Brock Change Skill 1, *Personal Vision*).

2. Publicize your *New Beginnings,* and set an example (Change Step 3).

3. Write down the specific parts of this change step, and make sure each person knows his or her part (Change Step 3, *New Beginnings*).

4. Reward risk-taking and small successes (Brock Change Skill 4, *Flexibility*).

Life in the Fast Lane

When life gets disrupted even in small ways, the male approach is to grab the reins. Women, on the other hand, will explore their options, negotiate, and try to avoid drastic consequences.

Let's look at Joanne. She's a suburban mother of three school-aged children. Her husband, Gene, is a pharmacist. Joanne has a part-time job at the local library. Both Joanne and Gene are active in their children's schools and community.

She's finally organized her life. Gene has to leave for work by 8:00 A.M. The bus gets to the bottom of the hill at 8:05, where it picks up the twins. At 8:15, Gene Jr. must be ready in his wheelchair for the bus that picks him up. This means that after Joanne has made sure the children are on their way, she has to be in the car to go to work by 8:30.

Imagine her chagrin when she got a notice that the school bus schedule was changing. Due to municipal budget cuts, the bus for the twins would no longer stop at the bottom of their hill. Instead, the twins would have to wait at another stop, on the other side of a busy highway. The bus would pick them up at 8:20, fifteen minutes later than usual.

Fortunately, Joanne and Gene had worked out the picture of the life they wanted to lead. This gave her some guiding principles she could use as she tried to rework her schedule around the new requirements. She identified the problem and how to get the twins to the new bus stop and make sure they were picked up. At the same time, she had to make sure Gene Jr. got on his bus and that she arrived at her job on time.

Because she had a focus point for her life, Joanne was able to bring some sense to the needed changes and how to set priorities. Joanne and Gene decided that the safety of their children and their getting a good education was the family's number-one priority.

But Joanne still felt frustrated about the situation, and she wanted to talk with her friends to see how they would handle it. Actually, she wanted to be able to vent her frustrations a bit before Gene got home. She realized he was uncomfortable when he saw her upset. So, she called her friend Salena and had a good venting session. Joanne emerged, feeling saner and ready to present the situation to Gene.

After talking with Gene, Joanne realized she needed to look to her strengths to be able to solve the problem. She had excellent relationships with administrators at her children's schools and had built solid contacts in the community. Then she thought, "I'm good at telephoning people and asking them how much flexibility they have. Why not use that to solve this problem?"

Women have a natural ability for reframing, in that they're more sensitive to their environments. They can also help others to look at old situations in new ways. Joanne thought she'd start her phone calls with Gene's school. Since it was a private school and they were paying for it, her needs would have more weight than with the twins' public school.

She rehearsed the approach she would take with the school principal. She was going to ask if Gene's pickup time could be a little earlier. She wanted to approach the situation with some solutions in mind, so she thought she'd suggest that Gene Jr. might be able to volunteer to do some extra work in the library. The earlier pickup time would mean he would now be getting to school a little earlier.

Using the Brock Method, Joanne made sure she went into the situation assuming there would be a positive outcome— not necessarily the one she had in mind, but one that would benefit all parties. She also primed herself to listen intently to make sure the principal was satisfied with the outcome. She didn't want to compromise her son's position in the school. Using what she learned from studying assertiveness, she made sure she outlined what she needed.

The call went very well. The principal not only agreed to the earlier pickup time, he agreed that he might have some duties in the library that Gene Jr. could take on.

Change Lessons from Joanne

1. Know where you're going and define the values that are most important to you (Brock Change Skill 1, *Personal Vision*).

2. Ask your partner for help, but realize his/her strengths and weaknesses (Brock Change Skill 3, *Emotional Resilience*).

3. Have a network of friends to call on for support in times of change (Brock Change Skill 3, *Emotional Resilience*).

4. Remember to use your strengths to solve the problems that change brings (Brock Change Skill 1, *Personal Vision*).

5. Act as if you'll have a positive outcome, and you're

more likely to have it (Brock Change Skill 5, *Self-Sense*).

6. Learn assertiveness techniques (Brock Change Skill 5, *Self-Sense*).

7. During a change, take a little extra time to notice the reaction of what you say on other people. Then you'll be able to course correct if needed (Brock Change Skill 2, *Reframing*).

A Serene Life, Interrupted

Dominick had lived in the same house for thirty years. He and his mother, Mrs. Garcia, had always enjoyed sitting on their patio and taking in the view from the adjacent park. They were appalled when their community decided to put up a large three-story building to house a conservation center. It was be right in front of their patio. Furthermore, it would take more than a year to build, causing further noise and disruption in their quiet lives. As much as they favored the aims of conservation, both feared their lives would never be the same. How could they adjust to the noise and chaos of the year of building? What would become of their quiet evenings of contemplation looking at the peaceful park? Dominick is a copyeditor, and he does most of his work at home. The year of noise would seriously affect his working conditions. He wanted to take immediate action. He thought about selling the house, even though he really loved it. He was complaining when his sister and her daughter came to visit on Sunday. His eight-year-old niece reacted strongly. "Why move from a place you really like?" she asked innocently. "Why not just make your house higher?" Everyone at first laughed at her naïveté. She was intuitively reframing the issue, as children, particularly girls, tend to do.

"Wait," said Dominick, "We've been thinking about renovating, why not just build another story on top, or at least a room? That could be my office, and we could build a deck to enjoy the evening sunsets." Once he got the idea, Dominick found it easy to work out the action. The Garcias had a builder price out the renovation, and they found a solution within their budget. Once they got the plans drafted, they had a copy framed and put it in a prominent place. It would remind them of how much nicer the house was going to be in a year. However, the house renovation only increased the disruption to come in the next year. What were Dominick and Mrs. Garcia to do? They made a pact that they would help each other through the difficult year. They became reframing buddies.

Mrs. Garcia also felt this was a good time to teach her son a life lesson, "Dominick, I'm old enough to justify a little rigidity, but you're only thirty years old," she said, "and you're becoming set in your ways. We eat at the same time, see the same people, and have the same outings as we did five years ago. Let's go on a campaign to increase our flexibility." Reluctantly, he said he'd try it. First of all, they decided to think of as many ways as possible to keep the noise and dirt from disrupting their lives. For Dominick's birthday, Mrs. Garcia said she was going to give him a pair of industrial earplugs that would diminish noise up to twenty-seven decibels. Then the Garcias asked the community to give them a copy of the construction schedule for the conservation building. It turned out that the crew wouldn't work on weekends. Since the family was hiring the crew for their own house renovation, they would be able to specify no weekend construction work. That would mean weekends would be a guaranteed quiet time. Dominick had a flexible work schedule, so he decided to take his weekend during the week and plan to be out of the house for two days while the crews were working. It would also signal a time for recovery. At his mother's urging, Dominick decided to take up tennis. He planned for lessons at the local YMCA, where there was a Thursday afternoon class for singles. The class would give him practice in flexibility and release some of his stress through regular physical activity. As a bonus, it would also give him the excitement of learning something new. Plus, it would have the advantage of letting him meet some other single people in the community. Mrs. Garcia also thought the same principle would work for her, so she decided to visit the local senior center and sign up for an exercise class and bridge lessons. Mrs. Garcia's request for her birthday gift was more laughter. This request forced both of them to think of what made them laugh. They both liked the musical comedy movies of the 1940s and 1950s, so they made up a list of the fifty-two they would rent, borrow, or buy. They'd have a movie every week during the construction period. This would be a way of rewarding themselves for getting through another week of noise and dirt.

Change Lessons from Dominick and Mrs. Garcia

1. Reframe problem situations. Think like a child, or—even better—listen to a child's view of your situation (Brock Change Skill 2, *Reframing*).
2. Find a reframing buddy (Brock Change Skill 2, *Reframing*).
3. Exercise your flexibility muscle (Brock Change Skill 4, *Flexibility*).
4. Keep a picture of your end goal in a prominent place so you see it every day (Brock Change Skill 1, *Personal Vision*).
5. Plan recovery time (Brock Change Skill 3, *Emotional Resilience*).

6. Build more laughter into your life (Brock Change Skill 3, *Emotional Resilience*).
7. Exercise regularly (Brock Change Skill 4, *Flexibility*).
8. Ask for help (Brock Change Skill 2, *Reframing*).
9. Research the facts on the change. It's easy to assume the worst (Brock Change Skill 2, *Reframing*).
10. Reward yourself for small wins (Brock Change Skill 4, *Flexibility*).
11. Break down big problems into smaller ones (Brock Change Skill 4, *Flexibility*).

The next chapter will address how stress can escalate when you have many changes going on at the same time. We'll show you how men and women cope in different ways. In addition, we'll examine the ways in which the stage of life affects the way a man or a woman handles change.

Chapter 17

Timing, Life Stages, and Changes for Men and Women

THE HEART OF MOST OF OUR PROBLEMS WITH CHANGE IS THAT we are in the middle of at least four major types of changes at any one point in time. Beyond that, there are also the minor changes to think about as well. Each day brings more change to our lives, and the common perception is true: The pace of change is accelerating. Although we do sometimes reach out for change, most change is visited upon us.

Today change is all around us. No matter what phase of life we're in, everybody at all times is experiencing some kind of change. You might be saying goodbye to a friend who has moved out of town. Maybe you're in the process of finding a new place to get really fresh produce. Maybe you're experiencing Change Step 3, *New Beginnings,* with the addition of a new person on your work team. Or maybe you're going through all these changes at the same time.

In a hierarchy like the workplace, it's easy for those who are making the change to forget that those people who are affected by it will also need time to work through the three steps of change. This can happen in a family too. Mom and Dad may have thought about making a change for a while before they spring it on the children. It's important in this case to give the children a chance to work through the change in their own way and time.

Delores and Steve Huff had been talking about the move to Chicago for several months before they told their girls. Delores and Steve had had time to think about why the change was necessary and to start thinking about what they'd be leaving. They also knew they were in control of the situation. The children didn't have the benefit of control, and they needed more time to even start absorbing the emotional repercussions of Change Step 1, *Say Goodbye*. Once Delores and Steve understood the steps that everyone needs to go through to change, they realized the children weren't acting up. They just needed a little time to catch up with the change.

Are men or women better at handling this multiplicity of changes? Research shows that women are better able to handle many changes at the same time. Men benefit from the male hormone, testosterone, which helps them focus better than women. But it interferes with their ability to juggle many changes at once.

As a kindergarten teacher, Rita told us that when she started teaching, she had every intention of creating a classroom that was free of gender bias. She was going to encourage boys to play with dolls and girls to build things. "However," she told us, "these five- and six-year-olds come with their gender imprinting already established. I could see it in the way they formed groups. One boy would become the leader and there would usually be two lieutenants in each class. There was a definite hierarchy among the boys in each class. "Girls were so much different. Any leader would be temporary. And they were so much more verbal, even to saying bad things about the leader to bring her down. Every day some girl was crying."

Emma and Jonathan Have a Runaway Success

As partners in a relatively new executive search business, Emma and Jonathan had very different backgrounds. That was one reason they made good partners. Emma had worked as a chief financial officer for ten years for a large nonprofit business. Jonathan had been on the marketing side of a software company.

When they met at a professional association committee, they got to know each other. Both had always had the dream of owning a business. To their delight, it's been a huge success. But they never thought success would bring so many problems. Emma is also in the midst of the changes that come with a young family, and Jonathan has the challenge of finishing his MBA degree. Emma finds she can manage the multiple priorities fairly well, better than Jonathan, but she needs his ability to focus when the business needs it. Most days she feels torn in many directions and she looks to him to take the necessary action.

Change Lessons from Emma and Jonathan

1. Men are naturally better at focusing to accomplish a task (Brock Change Skill 2, *Reframing*).
2. Women can use their natural flexibility to manage multiple priorities (Brock Change Skill 4, *Flexibility*).
3. Use the opposite gender's natural strengths to enhance your efforts (Brock Change Skill 2, *Reframing*).

A Caregiver's Dilemma

Laura has lived in the same town all her life. Even so, she has undergone many changes. She thought she had gone through the biggest change when her mother had a stroke and had to go into a nursing home. Even with the demands of her growing family, Laura managed to go to her mother's nursing home every day for three years. As a woman, she used her natural skill in being able to handle many responsibilities at once. Her husband, Bill, is amazed at how much she's able to do. He's happy that she leaves him alone to do his job of bringing in the money to support the family. Unfortunately, Laura's mother took a turn for the worse and died. Laura mourned and decided she'd keep her mother's generous spirit alive by distributing a piece of her extensive jewelry collection to each of her mother's many friends. As she did, some people said, "It's for the better, you'll have more time for your husband and children now." Bill tends to agree, but he's sensitive enough not to say so. He hopes she'll now have more time for him, not that he'd ever mention it. Bill asked Laura to attend one of our seminars with him. It was an easier way for him to bring up his emotional needs than talking. He knows that Laura has to take time to mourn her mother, but she'll eventually need a new way to structure the day.

Change Lessons from Laura and Bill

1. Part of the mourning process is to keep the loved one's spirit with you (Change Step 3, *New Beginnings*).
2. It's also important to fill the time you spent with them with other rewarding activities (Brock Change Skill 3, *Emotional Resilience*).

3. Women are naturally better at juggling many responsibilities than most men (Brock Change Skill 4, *Flexibility*).

Living in a World of Change

Nadine was very young at heart when we first met her, with fantasies of a knight in shining armor who would carry her off into the sunset. She met Frank while finishing her college degree. It was love at first sight, and soon after her father was giving her away at the all-white wedding of her dreams. A year later, they were proud parents of little Jules, and Frank was working hard to finish medical school.

Fast-forward thirty-five years. Nadine's mother has died, and her father has decided to move into Nadine and Frank's neighborhood. Frank has taken early retirement from his medical practice and plans for a life of golf and travel. Jules has decided he doesn't want to be married anymore. The fantasy of marriage disappeared a long time ago, but Nadine has seen many more realistic dreams become reality, like owning a house.

As a woman, Nadine has already had to say a lot of good-byes, and she feels she's been pretty good at it. She has made the symbolic gesture of taking a lot of her late mother's favorite furniture into her house. Nadine felt that the gesture really helped her mother's spirit enrich her life. Frank, as a man, thought that was a little silly, but he understood that it was just one of the ways women need to cope with change.

When Nadine brought up the subject of what they could do to help her father get over his mourning, Frank, again savvy to the ways of women managing change, was able to listen. He volunteered to play golf with his father-in-law at least once a week and encouraged him to get involved in some community affairs. Then came the bombshell of Jules's divorce. Frank tried to put himself in Nadine's place. He worried that Nadine would be afraid that he might do the same thing—just walk out on her. But that was not Nadine's reaction at all. Instead, she was asking herself what she had done wrong in raising Jules, that he would leave his marriage so abruptly. Nadine must learn that Jules's decisions are not her worry.

Change Lessons from Nadine
1. It's better to have dreams than fantasies for your life (Brock Change Skill 5, *Emotional Self-Sense*).
2. Keeping a favorite object helps the mourning process (Change Step 1, *Say Goodbye*).
3. Value a man who will listen. It's rarely a natural talent (Brock Change Skill 2, *Reframing*).
4. Her worry is not necessarily his (Brock Change Skill 2, *Reframing*).
5. His worry is not necessarily hers (Brock Change Skill 2, *Reframing*).

One Change Opens Up Many Possibilities

Albert had been a bachelor for many years, moving from one woman to another while he climbed the corporate ladder at a large investment bank. He managed a high-risk fund worth billions of dollars, but he lived in a small studio apartment. He never traveled except to go to conferences where he was to be a speaker.

Grace was determined to marry Albert, and she finally got him to take the big plunge. Wise to the ways in which men approach change, Grace gradually helped Albert realize his dream of opening up his own business. She found a new apartment for them and quickly made it a place where potential clients loved to come. Albert had a good voice and had been in a men's choir for years, but Grace helped him see he would enjoy singing even more if he took lessons. Then she started devoting some time to a major vacation every year, an opportunity for both of them to widen their horizons. "I'm amazed," Albert told us, "that so many good things could come into my life in such a short time." What he isn't saying is that he opened himself up to change, with Grace's help.

Change Lessons from Grace and Albert

1. It's easy to worry about negative changes to come, but many unanticipated changes are positive ones (Brock Change Skill 2, *Reframing*).
2. Women are more attuned than men to bringing about changes that have emotional weight (Brock Change Skill 3, *Emotional Resilience*).

Judy's Story

When Judy talked to us, it was after her father had passed away. She told me that she now faced a number of changes in her life, and since she was in her late fifties, she was unsure if she could face them all at once. The first change Judy faced was not so much the death of her father as the loss of the role of caregiver. Her father was a very old man when he passed, well into his nineties, and he had led a good life. Everyone who knew him was sad to see him go, but Judy and her family realized that the wonderful memories their father had given them would be theirs for the rest of their lives. No, Judy realized, the problem wasn't so much the loss of her father. It was not being needed to make the trip to the nursing home every day to see how she could be of help. Judy had gotten used to helping her father and thinking of him often. Now what was she going to do all day?

Another change in Judy's life threatened to change her relationship with her husband. Paul was an engineer who had worked at a large company in their town for many years. He was a dedicated worker and in demand as a top engineer in a growing science, so throughout his career he had made a routine of working late at the office. He also was required to travel extensively in his job.

One big change frequently comes with several others. Sometimes he would be away from home for ten days or more at a stretch. Judy had become used to this routine over the years. She didn't mind it too much because she realized that Paul was working for his family. Besides, Judy was busy with the kids and her own job.

But then Paul retired, and suddenly he was home all day. He worked as a consultant out of his home office, and that kept him busy, but he was still there. Although Judy still loved and admired her husband, the sudden closeness was difficult for both of them to handle. He was on the computer just when she wanted to go online. He would be using the telephone when Judy wanted to talk to her friend Emily. She ran the vacuum cleaner just when he wanted quiet to concentrate on his engineering equations. The change in their lifestyles was beginning to affect their relationship. But Judy had another worry. With his retirement, Paul finally had the freedom to assess his life. Judy was concerned that her husband might take a cue from his ex-son-in-law, with whom he had been very close, and look for a new wife. Judy knew in her heart of hearts that this was not going to happen, but that didn't stop her from worrying about it anyway.

There Judy was, at a time in life when people are supposed to be relaxing and enjoying their grandchildren, suddenly getting hit with three profound changes in her life. Judy was smart enough to know that these changes would certainly alter the relationship she had with her husband, but she wanted to know how the change could be a positive one.

Judy sat down and used elements of the Brock Method to sort out the stages of change and to find ways to make change work for her, rather than just passively waiting for bad things to happen. She took our advice about looking at each change independently to see what natural skills she had to cope with it. With her father's death, she realized that she not only had to mourn him, but also mourn the loss of the purpose his caretaking had given her life.

> When dealing with multiple changes, take a look at each one independently and how to cope with it.

Judy took her cues from the tips on Change Step 1, *Say Goodbye*. She reflected on all the pleasure she had gotten from going to the nursing home to visit her father. She enjoyed the break from her chaotic day, and just being with the elderly and ill made her slow down. Nobody moves very fast in the daily routine of a nursing home. Then she started to ask herself an important question. "Is there something else I can do at the nursing home that would give me a break from home and also be valuable?" She was starting to move into the next step of change by trying out new ways to fulfill the satisfaction she'd had as a caregiver.

Next, she tackled the change of suddenly having her husband at home all the time. She realized that part of what was making things so difficult was that he had a very different approach to handling the change. He was looking for something to keep him active and to give him the same ego satisfaction he had gotten from his job. However, it was just about all she could do to manage her frustration at having him constantly underfoot. She used the Brock Method to think about how she could be more assertive and express her frustration to him. Although she was hesitant, he was quite willing to hear her out. He said, "Why didn't you say something sooner?" They were even able to brainstorm some possible ways to give each other a little more space. What came up was that he had always dreamed of making the attic into a writer's loft. Judy agreed to clear out the twenty years' worth of junk that had accumulated there. Paul began contacting contractors and drawing up plans for his new space. Having had good success with talking about the space issue, Judy decided to take a chance and bring up her fears about Paul's doing what Terry's husband had done. Paul reacted with surprise. "No chance," he said, "I've just never been the kind of man who gives up. Look at that job. I probably should have left earlier. Instead, I hung around until they literally had to throw me out."

Change Lessons from Judy and Paul

1. When confronting multiple changes, look at them separately (Brock Change Skill 2, *Reframing*).
2. Focus on what you can control (Brock Change Skill 3, *Emotional Resilience*).
3. Voice your fears to someone who can do something about them (Brock Change Skill 2, *Reframing*).
4. Acknowledge what you've lost (Change Step 1, *Say Goodbye*).

Men, Women, and Change Throughout a Lifetime

Change can also mean different things during the many stages of a lifetime. Men and women look at themselves through different lenses as they move through life. We like to do it with a smile.

Age	A Woman Looks in the Mirror	A Man Looks in the Mirror
8	She sees a fairy tale princess.	He sees his sports hero.
15	She sees fat/pimples/gawky and feels like staying home.	He sees a young man; he wants to be older, more mature.
20	She sees fat/pimples/gawky, but goes out anyway.	He sees someone the world wants, young and strong, a future ahead of him.
30	She sees nothing she likes but is too busy to bother.	He sees success and concentrates on getting ahead in life, career, etc.
40	She sees nothing she likes but says "At least I'm clean," and goes anyway.	He sees less hair and some graying hair and starts looking for something else, but doesn't know what it is.
50	She sees a woman and goes out to live her life.	He sees gray hair and figures he'd better do something quick before it's all over.
60	She sees a woman and says, "If they could only see me now."	He sees only gray hair, thinks this is his last shot at life, and enjoys the sweetness.
70	She's happy to see a living, breathing woman and enjoys her life.	He's glad to see any hair, figures what is done is done, and proceeds to enjoy it.
80	She puts a flower in her hair and goes out to enjoy herself.	He's amazed he's still alive, spends a lot of time looking back at what he did, and still enjoys his hair.
90	Can't see, so doesn't worry about it!	He doesn't bother with a mirror at all, spends a lot of time sleeping, but in his dreams he still has hair.

Men, Women, Change, and the Ages of Romantic Life

The differing male and female lenses are even more divergent when it comes to romance. No wonder it sometimes seems that there is no getting us together.

Age	A Woman's Romantic Life	A Man's Romantic Life
8	She doesn't care about boys.	He hates girls.
15	She likes boys and is trying to figure out what they want.	He's interested in girls but is afraid of them.
20	Men fight for her attention.	He likes girls and isn't afraid anymore.
30	She can hear the biological clock ticking.	Women want him now.
40	It's now or never to find that special one.	Women want him even more now.
50	She's feeling the heat from younger women.	He's really in charge of the social scene.
60	She understands why women get plastic surgery.	He feels like being with one special woman.
70	She'd like to find a man who could drive at night.	He's happy to be with any woman.
80	She'd like to find a man who could drive.	He's happy to be with anybody.
90	She's happy just to talk.	He's happy to be.

As the course of life unfolds, the challenges that we encounter and the changes that we must face are very different for each age. Moreover, it is not too surprising that men and women react to these life changes in profoundly different ways. After all, men and women have varied roles in our society. These roles are defined in many cases by natural biology, but there is also a strong component of societal conformity in everyone. Our differences are particularly evident in the mating and courting rituals that we commonly call romance.

Chapter 18

Conclusions: Changing Together

ONE OF THE GREAT CHALLENGES FOR ANYONE IN A RELATIONSHIP—whether it's romantic, work, or family—is how to react and respond to the other person. Human beings are complex and usually exasperating creatures with a wide repertoire of emotions and actions. It's what makes drama a three-thousand-year-old art. It's what drives love stories and soap operas on television, in the movies, and in every other kind of entertainment. It's called life. We live it. We reach out to another person to live with us. And we hold on to others for love, security, pleasure, jobs, family, and loyalty. The great challenge we face in everyday life is to make these relationships that are at the center of our lives work successfully.

Change is the great constant in life. It is always there. Change is also the great challenge to our relationships. A new boss comes on the job, and suddenly you are asked to perform in different ways. A child leaves for college, and soon your life with your longtime spouse is different in many silent ways. You move to another city, and everything in your life feels different, including your family. Every time we experience change, our relationship with other people is altered, molded, and shaped in a different way. Our thesis here is that a person can anticipate and understand change and the people involved in it to build a more productive and satisfying life. In other words, if you are prepared for change, it can be used to strengthen and deepen human bonds.

Now that we have looked at many examples of change, and how men and women can make change work for them in their own very positive ways, it is vital at this point that we put it all together. If we all, men and women alike, can reach for understanding of each other as we confront life's changes, then we can build stronger, more fruitful bonds with each other. So we may ask, what does all this mean to me? How can I get started? How can I take the understanding of my partner to a new level of harmony?

We started by showing you how men and women are structured differently. Evolution and development have created a female brain and a male brain. There are of course many differences in the way these organs are constructed and how our minds confront the outside world. Of the myriad of variations that arise in the milieu of genetics and physiology, one of the most prominent is the anatomy of connections. The female brain has a larger and thicker connector between the two hemispheres than the male. One example that we discussed in Chapter 3 is that this brain structure makes emotions permeate more of a woman's life than they do a man's life.

This anatomical structure is believed to create different neural nets resulting in the general observation that men and women process language and visual spatial tasks in different places in their brains. Also, we've seen that the male hormone testosterone predisposes men to different behavior patterns during change than do the female hormones.

Biology translates to behavior. This is a truism in our world. Physiology and anatomy are the engines of our response to the outside world, and even as we accept free will and individual choice, we know that in some respects all of us are conditioned to act in certain ways when challenged by change. We have concluded that when change happens, men are generally geared to take action and women to reach out, talk, and come to a more unstructured solution. In human history, it's easy to see that men had to develop focus to be effective hunters. Women, on the other hand, had to be more resourceful when they were protecting their children, managing the home, and creating backup food for the days when their men didn't come back with a kill.

The more we know about the ways in which the opposite gender is predisposed to react in the face of change, the better we can live, work, and play together. This book is structured so you can look specifically into the eight major changes of life and see how ordinary men and women have successfully coped with change and how they've used their understanding of the opposite sex to manage effectively. You've met specific individuals from our research and practice who have navigated the sometimes stormy waters of the sexes in marriage and divorce, dating, parenting, moving, changing health, changing finances, working, and external tragedies and disturbances. They have made change work for them and their partners by understanding the structure of changes in their lives and those of their partners.

How Men Make Change Work; How Women Make Change Work

This book contains our observations and research on how men and women are different in handling the three major steps of change as they arose in our careers of teaching, research, and writing. Remember those steps for change: *Say Goodbye, Move Through the Middles,* and *New Beginnings.* By now you should be ready to apply them in your own lives. We've also given you suggestions for managing each step of the way. During our journey through change, we also focused on how to use the Brock Method to develop the skills you'll need to cope with change. There were illustrations of how men and women exhibit these skills in different ways and how real people have used them in their lives.

Of the five skills, men have a natural talent for creating a personal vision and tend to have a stronger sense of self. Women can do both, but approach it from a more complex set of strengths and passions and a less traditional sense of self. Women often have the advantage in reframing, emotional resilience, and flexibility. One of the most important lessons to be taken from this book is that although men and women handle change differently, both sexes experience lots of change in their lives and can most often deal with it successfully. If each gender can understand how his or her partner deals with the change at hand, then that relationship can be strengthened by the change, rather than hurt by it. As we go through the changes in our lives, we make a series of small decisions that take us through to the result. If those decisions are guided by an understanding of the human response of men and women and how they can best get through that change, then our lives will be infinitely more productive and happy with our partners.

Refer to any of the following resources to further your exploration into the ways of change.

Resources

This section lists some of the more useful reference material we have found for further development in making change work.

William Bridges, *Managing Transitions: Making the Most of Change, 2nd Edition* (Perseus, 2003).

Pierce J. Howard, *The Owner's Manual for the Brain: Everyday Applications from Mind-Brain Research* (Bard Press, 2000).

Susan Jeffers, *Feel the Fear and Do It Anyway* (Fawcett, 1985).

Ann Moir and David Jessel, *Brain Sex: The Real Difference Between Men and Women* (Dell, 1993).

Steven Pinker, *The Blank Slate: The Denial of Human Nature* (Viking, 2002).

Steven Pinker, *How the Mind Works* (Norton, 1999).

Appendix

Change Tables

In the Introduction, we told you that *Men Head East, Women Turn Left* would answer the following questions:

1. How do men and women approach change differently?
2. What are the three steps we all need to go through in reacting to change? How are men and women likely to handle each one?
3. What are the five skills for making change work? Which are easiest for women? Which are easiest for men?
4. How do men and women approach the eight major life changes?
5. What can we learn from each other?
6. Why aren't we communicating?

We like to keep our promises, and we really do think that we've answered all of these questions through:

- Our discussion of the different ways that men and women face change
- Our explanation of the three necessary Change Steps and of the Brock Method for improving your change skills
- The many real-life examples from our research on men and women dealing with change, both alone and together

In this appendix, we provide tables related to each of the first four questions. These tables summarize all the essential concepts, tell a quick version of the personal stories we've used for illustration, and give the most important lessons that you can take away to deal with change in your own life.

What about questions 5 and 6? As we've said throughout the book, when men and women begin to learn that they approach change differently—and that they can make use of the best aspects of the other gender's change style—they will avoid misunderstandings and improve relationships in many areas of their lives. As for why we aren't communicating yet, we hope that this book will contribute to opening up a dialogue between men and women on how to best face—together—the increasingly fast-paced changes of life today.

Men Change, Women Change: Essential Differences

How Men Approach Change	How Women Approach Change
More inward and focused	More likely to reach out for help and research options
Dependent on a traditional structure	
	Handle change in a less structured way
Find it hard to express emotions	
Not naturally gifted in resilience and flexibility	Able to express emotions about change
Self-confidence comes more naturally	Find it easier to be emotionally resilient and flexible
May be too impulsive in desire to take action	Need time to grieve and talk about the losses change brings
May forget to consult with partner when necessary	Can get stuck in thinking through what to do in times of change
Find it easier to fall back on already tried methods	May forget to think about own needs in helping others during change

Examples:

Tom

Change challenge: Moving into a new house (with Sara)

Response: Leapt into action; put up all the picture frames

Sara

Change challenge: Moving into a new house

Response: Considered each room and visualized how it would look best

Lessons:

- When immediate action is required and the right thing to do is clear, the masculine style works best.
- When the outcome is less apparent and you have time to adjust, the feminine approach works better.

The Three Change Steps

Change Step 1: Say Goodbye

Summary:

- Saying goodbye is the most important and most commonly overlooked step of change.
- Women find it easier to talk with others and take the time to say the necessary goodbyes.
- Men find it easier to act without much talking.
- Women need to talk with others before committing to action.

Examples:

Marjorie and Sam

Change challenge: Bankruptcy of their clothing store

Response: Sam immediately took a job organizing closing of stores; Marjorie put together a farewell party for the store and selected keepsakes from the house they had to sell.

Gayle and Joe

Change challenge: Death of Gayle's sister in car accident

Response: Gayle grieved with the many relatives and helped her brother-in-law and nephew; her friend Joe pitched in to help with funeral arrangements.

Vivien

Change challenge: Death of husband after long marriage

Response: Expanded her social circle from couples only to include singles and mixed groups

Lessons:

- Accept the reality of emotional losses.
- Create a symbol or a ritual for what is lost.

- Define what is over and what will continue.
- Be willing to discuss losses openly.
- Understand the different needs others may have for saying goodbye.
- Make use of the male ability for decisive action when needed, and the female emphasis on considering the emotional repercussions when appropriate.

Change Step 2: Move Through the Middles

Summary:

- This step requires taking control and getting through an awkward period fast.
- Signs that you are in this stage include confusion and a feeling of being out of control.
- Getting through this step requires making a bridge to the new situation and trying temporary ways of coping.
- Men find this step easier because they are used to just doing what is necessary.

Examples:

Marjorie and Sam

Change challenge: Adjusting to Sam's new job organizing bankruptcy sales

Response: Marjorie used her expertise in store displays to make his project a success.

Vivien

Change challenge: Moving through her period of mourning for her husband

Response: Went to widow's support groups to learn how others coped; researched options for staying in her large house

Dick and Rosa

Change challenge: Coping with the limited authority given officers of their community casino

Response: Dick identified high-priority items and moved on them; Rosa made sure rules were followed and human issues were at the top of the list.

Lessons:

- Make it through this stage as quickly as possible.
- Get the essentials taken care of safely, even if it's temporary.
- Focus on what you can control.
- Set short-range goals that are achievable.
- Take calculated risks when necessary to go beyond the usual.

Change Step 3: New Beginnings

Summary:

- This step is the adoption of new behaviors that reflect the changed situation.
- Both women and men are good at this, but tend to express it in different ways.
- Women tend to visualize the future and then express that vision to others.
- Men rely on action and work hard to set an example that others can follow.
- This stage has begun when trust and optimism start to build.

Examples:

Marjorie and Sam

Change challenge: Making their new business a permanent part of their lives

Response: Marjorie used detailed records of customers from old business to start a mail-order offshoot of their new business.

Gayle

Change challenge: Incorporating larger role of her nephew whose mother died into her life

Response: She gave him a room in her home; organized a new studio space for her work as an artist to maintain her own privacy.

Marisa

Change challenge: Losing a substantial amount of weight and keeping it off

Response: She set non-food rewards for each ten pounds lost and also for each month that she stays at her desired weight.

Lessons:

- Paint a clear, specific picture of the future.
- Explain to others the reasoning behind the New Beginning.
- Recognize your small successes.
- Make use of the elements of your previous situation in your new one if possible.
- Find new practices and structures to solidify the advances you've already achieved.

The Brock Method for Increasing Your Change Skills

Of the five tools presented here, men have more natural talent for creating a personal vision and often have a stronger sense of self. Women tend to have the advantage in reframing, emotional resilience, and flexibility. However, everyone can improve individual abilities for each of these change skills.

Change Skill 1: Create a Personal Vision

Summary:

- Without a clear idea of where you want to go, successful change is impossible.
- A major change in your environment is often a signal that it's time to revisit your personal vision.
- You can use the Mix 'n' Match Tool at the end of Chapter 8 to help you in starting to form your vision.

Examples:

Penny

Change challenge: Desire to help in her community

Response: She combined her ability to speak French and love for tennis to formulate a plan for taking local teenagers to a tennis camp in France.

Henry

Change challenge: Caught in a dead-end job in a bland suburb

Response: He used his ability in tax and accounting to get a new job as the CFO of a Colorado ski resort.

Mary

Change challenge: Retired after twenty-five years at the same firm

Response: She decided to find a way to combine her knowledge and love of baking with her desire to help people live healthier lives.

Lessons:
- Only passions, great passions, can elevate us to great things.
- Your personal vision of the future should pass the 3-M test; make it Memorable, Motivating, and Meaningful.
- When deciding on your personal vision, engage the mind and heart wherever possible.

Change Skill 2: Reframing
Summary:
- This change skill requires you to look at yourself and your life as if you were seeing it for the first time.
- When change happens, we tend to close ourselves into our group and give little consideration to other points of view at the time when we need to most.
- Use "the naive eye" to find new opportunities in your environment for managing change.
- Women have a natural ability when it comes to reframing because they are naturally more sensitive to their environments.

Examples:
Peggy
Change challenge: Difficulty in conveying to others what it was she did as a research technologist

Response: After being asked by her daughter what she did, she realized that she could best explain her job by imagining how to say it to a six-year-old.

Lisa

Change challenge: Moved from California to New York

Response: She realized that her sunny California optimism was not being taken seriously enough, and that she had to express herself in a more measured, careful way.

Lessons:

- During periods of change, take an extra second after you've spoken or acted to see what the reaction has been.
- Develop your listening skills; women come by this more naturally, but everyone can improve.
- Taking a new perspective on obstacles in your life can open up room for creativity and opportunity.

Change Skill 3: Develop Your Emotional Resilience

Summary:

- Stress and change are not always negative; at the right levels, they stimulate and lead to growth.
- People who have emotional resilience find it easier to take change as a positive.
- Women find it easier to address their emotions and develop the emotional resilience that change requires.
- Consider all the different elements of your life to see if you are devoting at least some time to each.
- We can train for the stress of change both physically—with diet and exercise—and emotionally.
- One of the best ways to deal with stress is to laugh as often as you can.

Examples:

The Huff family

Change challenge: Dealing with the stresses of their move from Chicago to Houston

Response: They decided to increase the amount of time they spent together as a family for three months; they set aside a time on Sunday afternoon for sharing stories of success and failure; and each member promised to bring in at least one thing to make them all laugh during this family gathering.

Lessons:
- Balance work, fun, family, friends, and the other important elements of your life.
- Cultivate people and activities that make you laugh.
- Plan recovery time for dealing with emotionally stressful changes.

Change Skill 4: Increase Your Flexibility

Summary:
- This skill requires that you be willing to look out for new approaches and new things to learn.
- Men are target-focused; they've been directed by society and genes to concentrate on one goal, which can hamper flexibility.
- Women are open to more unstructured solutions and can be flexible in trying them out.
- As Darwin noted, the species that are the most flexible in the face of change have the greatest chance for survival.

Examples:

George

Change challenge: Wanted to lose 100 pounds, which seemed impossible

Response: He practiced increasing his flexibility by going to unfamiliar golf courses, which provided helpful exercise, and by taking a course in nutrition at his local community college.

Lessons:

- Becoming flexible in small things can increase your capability for flexibility during large changes.
- If we don't practice our flexibility, big goals can seem so daunting that we will refuse to even try.
- Concentrate on small immediate goals that lead to the measurable success of the larger goal.

Change Skill 5: Increase Your Self-Sense

Summary:

- It takes a strong sense of yourself not to be buffeted about by winds of change.
- Our data show that it is in sense of self where women are weakest compared to men.
- A man's natural approach to increasing his sense of self includes complimenting himself on his good qualities and accomplishments.
- If people can strengthen their self-confidence, they will usually weather change more effectively.
- One way to increase your self-confidence is to form a Dream Team: a group of people who gather regularly to help one another handle life changes.

Examples:

Meredith

Change challenge: Wanted a promotion and a salary increase in her job in the competitive business of investment banking

Response: She defined what she wanted; she assembled facts on what typical salaries were for her position; she compiled all the positive things she had done for the organization; and she found a way to appeal to the motivations of her superiors in order to move toward her goals.

Lessons:

- Take the time to compliment yourself on your good qualities and accomplishments.
- To allow the compliments of others to register, repeat every compliment (to yourself) several times until it registers internally.
- Listen carefully to criticism, but decide on your own whether to accept it, depending on whether it's accurate and well motivated.
- Act as if you'll have a positive outcome and you're more likely to have it.

The Eight Major Life Changes

In responding to the significant challenges of change in these areas of life, people need to be sure that they don't neglect any of the three essential Change Steps, and that they work to improve their Change Skills as needed.

Life Situation 1: Marriage and Divorce

Summary:

- Simple differences cause many marriages to run up on the rocks.
- Couples should bring their feelings of loss out into the open and be specific about what each person misses from the old life before marriage, or, in the case of divorce, from the good parts of their marriage.

Examples:

Deborah and Mike

Change challenge: Deborah was an early bird, while Mike always wanted to stay up and go out; once they were married, it was difficult to get their lives in sync.

Response: They acknowledged what each missed about their lives before marriage; they then set up a Tuesday night "date" and a morning brunch once a month; and they worked on creative ways to enhance their new rituals.

Angela and Byron

Change challenge: Unable to communicate to each other the difficulties they faced in the changes brought about by marriage, they faced a second change in life as they divorced.

Response: Angela made a list of the good and bad in her marriage to Byron; she had her engagement ring reset into a different ring as a symbol of the ending of her marriage; and she resolved to make sure laughter and communication with her friends were part of her newly single life. Byron worked on resetting his personal vision and making changes in his career; he reframed his thinking about divorce to see it not simply as a failure; and he resolved to become more emotionally resilient and more patient in potential future romantic relationships.

Lessons:
- Accept the reality of emotional losses.
- It can be helpful to create a symbol for what you have lost.
- In any change, the Middles are messy, and you want to get through them fast.
- Find a place for laughter in your new life after a major change such as divorce.
- Consider change as a chance to learn, and gain a better sense of self.

Life Situation 2: Dating and Courtship
Summary:
- Women, more often than men, consult others about relationships, look for support from friends, and seek advice before taking action.
- Men may be less flexible when confronting the changes that relationships create in their lives.

Examples:
David and Celeste
Change challenge: After they began dating, she wanted him to spend weekends at her new country home, while he wanted to spend them in the city with his friends.
Response: David realized that spending time in the country was Celeste's way of seeing if they were compatible, so he

agreed to do it once a month if she agreed to spend one weekend a month in the city getting to know his friends. Celeste understood that she had to balance time with David and with her friends, and they also used a shared interest in tennis to draw them closer together.

Angela

Change challenge: Beginning to date again after her divorce while starting a new life in Hong Kong

Response: She asked a woman friend to go through the Mix 'n' Match tool to help define her personal vision and also to be her "dating coach"; and she developed a plan for varying her opportunities to meet someone and to avoid becoming too involved in her work.

Byron

Change challenge: Finding a way to focus on having a successful relationship after dating casually for several years after his divorce

Response: He decided to get to know some women more slowly through e-mail correspondence before meeting them in the more stressful environment of a traditional date; and he made an effort to meet women who could understand and share his passion for his business.

Lessons:

- Men in particular may need to work on their ability to listen and to be flexible.
- Women may find it necessary to tone down a natural inclination to accommodate others during change.
- Couples in the early stages of a relationship should make time for a transition period, the Middles, to take pressure off the relationship.

- Use dating as a chance to get to know yourself better.
- Learn to put dating disasters into perspective.
- Reframe the search phase of dating as an activity you can combine with something else.
- Dating is difficult, so reward yourself at each new step you take.

Life Situation 3: Family Life

Summary:

- In general, women are better at coping with changes in family situations.
- Men often need more structure and regulation when organizing their lives after a new child.

Examples:

Jose and Valerie

Change challenge: Dealing with the many changes brought by having their first baby

Response: Valerie understood that their old way of life would change forever with a child; Jose initially assumed that things could go on as before, but eventually found the temporary solution of requesting a work assignment closer to their home so that he could spend more time with the baby.

Sheila

Change challenge: Trying to fulfill her responsibilities as the single mother of two teenaged girls while pursuing her dream of becoming a writer

Response: Sheila found a job that began at 10 A.M., and her daughters pitched in to allow her to work on her novel from 7:30 to 9:30 every morning.

Lily and Leon

Change challenge: Finding a way to handle the issues raised by the increased health-care needs of aging parents

Response: Leon quickly acted after their father had a stroke to find an assisted-living home for their parents; Lily suggested they move more slowly, and together they came up with a solution that preserved more of their parents' independence and allowed them to stay in their own home.

Lessons:

- Many people expect only negative changes to be difficult, but positive changes such as having a child require just as much adaptation.
- In a partnership, use the feminine strength for saying goodbye, and then switch to the male strength of being able to quickly get through the Middles with direct action.
- A major life change is a perfect time to check life balance and improve your emotional resilience.
- Think about work as a way to fulfill more than money needs, and reframe its place in your life.
- Within your family, practice what you preach and make your dreams a priority.
- Think beyond the stereotypical response to change to one that is beneficial to all parties.

Life Situation 4: Moving

Summary:

- Men are more comfortable when the move is structured, and they don't like to talk much about details.
- Women like to have time to think through what their lifestyle is going to be in the new situation.
- Men are less imaginative than women in realistically

visualizing (rather than fantasizing) ways in which their lives could improve and are less willing to deal with the details that change almost always requires.

- Women are more open to the creative possibilities of a life change such as a move and will take time to find them.

Examples:

Lynn and Max

Change challenge: Handling the culture shock and change caused by Lynn's job being transferred to Paris

Response: They rented out the house in Atlanta they both loved to hold onto some of their past; Max took the change as an opportunity to reframe his thinking about his career and found a position in Paris that made use of his experience as a corporate lawyer.

Richard and Stacie

Change challenge: His job frequently changes location due to promotion and their family has had to move several times.

Response: Stacie creates goodbye rituals for each place that they have to leave, such as a farewell party and collecting e-mail addresses; in the new location, they buy a similar home, with rooms painted in similar colors to add some familiarity to their surroundings.

Ralph and Natalie

Change challenge: Adjusting to the changing character of their neighborhood, specifically their new next-door neighbors from India

Response: After some initial reluctance from Ralph, they met their neighbors with the open attitude of trying to learn about another culture and reframe their thinking about their own culture.

Louise

Change challenge: At the age of eighty, moving into a retirement home

Response: She became involved in some programs at the local seniors' center to shake up her routine; and she took a hand in choosing the decoration of her new room to make it seem more like her home.

Lessons:
- Allow your partner to react to your changes in his or her own way.
- Develop a process for getting through the Middles fast.
- Incorporate some elements of your previous surroundings into your new ones.
- Create rituals for saying goodbye.
- Men and women react to change on different time schedules.
- It takes time to handle major changes, so you should be patient with yourself and others undergoing change.
- Take on new interests at every stage of your life.

Life Situation 5: Health
Summary:
- Faced with the need to make a change for medical reasons, men tend to take decisive action, such as joining a gym, or else they go to the opposite extreme and choose not to hear the advice.
- Women are more likely to turn to diet and subtle life changes when faced with health questions.

- Women are also more likely to look to others for help and counsel, such as to a support group of people with similar problems.
- Men may just try to work through their health problems without articulating their needs very often.

Examples:

Peter

Change challenge: Being diagnosed with diabetes at a checkup around his fortieth birthday

Response: At his wife's insistence, he went to a specialist to create a vision of how he would need to modify his life; he then reframed his thinking about his work in the family garment business to change his position to one requiring shorter hours and less travel.

John

Change challenge: Changing his lifestyle after suffering a mild heart attack

Response: He left his high-stress corporate position and took on a temporary position as a consultant to get him through the Middles; he then used the Mix 'n' Match Tool to decide on a new direction and ended up starting a new small business with a partner that allowed him to spend time with his two teenaged sons.

Janet

Change challenge: Finding out she had breast cancer

Response: She immediately began talking with others who had had a similar illness; she researched all her treatment options; and she formulated a medical and psychological recovery plan.

Lessons:
- When big changes happen, take time to formulate the question of exactly what it is that you want.
- Ask for help, and listen carefully to others.
- During change, reach out, communicate more, and express trust.
- Take calculated risks to get through the Middles fast.
- Be specific about what you want from your life.
- Your partner is not likely to handle your change the way you do.
- Find out all you can about how to solve your change challenge, do it, and then let go of the anxiety.
- Create positive goals and timetables for them.

Life Situation 6: Finances

Summary:
- When financial change occurs, such as a drop in the stock market, men can take it in stride more quickly and move along.
- Women can take a more analytical approach and become focused on the details, while men may be more focused on the end result.

Examples:

Suzanne and Jack

Change challenge: Finding a way to organize their finances after moving to an area where Jack has a high-salary job, but expenses are also high

Response: Jack jumped right in and bought an expensive home; Suzanne consulted with many people to find a way to put together the house's financing; and she then made a plan for finding a job for herself that would allow her to pick her daughter up after school.

Joy

Change challenge: Starting retirement on a relatively small income

Response: She bought her computer from work and set up a Web site on the game of bridge, her longtime passion; she cut out all nonessential expenses, such as owning a car in the city when she no longer had to commute to work.

Lessons:

- Reframe financial challenges as opportunities to find new sources of income.
- Don't let your frustration at your partner's financial style interfere with the approaches that are successful for you.
- Acting fast is one financial strategy, and so is doing thorough research; they are complementary, depending on the situation.
- Open yourself up to learn new things at every age.
- Explore your passions without worrying about what others think.
- When one stage of your life is over, say goodbye and get on with what's next.

Life Situation 7: The Workplace

Summary:

- In a turbulent work situation, women have an easier time adjusting to some change because they are less invested in the traditional work structure.
- Men can be more resistant to change, and they may resort more to falling back on traditional hierarchies.
- Women have traditionally had to use the male change management strategy of fast definitive action in order to succeed in business.

- As organizations become more team-based, female change management strategies are becoming more effective.

Examples:

Katharine

Change challenge: Being appointed as team leader for a group to create a name and package for a new product

Response: She reached out to the creators of the product and others in the organization for information and support; she made efforts to get the members of the team to know one another and to resolve any personal issues that they might have; and she determined to have the group work to define clearly their goals and time frame.

John

Change challenge: As a major league pitcher, finding new ways to get hitters out when his fastball loses effectiveness

Response: After some failures and initial resistance, he developed the flexibility to work with a pitching coach to develop a good curve and slider.

Rita and Phil

Change challenge: Finding ways to lay off employees when necessary that are the most comfortable for everyone

Response: Phil drew on Rita's experience in creating good-bye rituals to devise a system where each person leaving the company is given a small token and given the sense that they are all valued alumni of the organization.

Lorraine

Change challenge: Her law firm was being taken over by a large European firm

Response: She welcomed the changes her new bosses brought to a traditional structure, and she reached out to them to see how their management strategies could work in her firm.

Ramon

Change challenge: Breaking up a thirteen-year-long business partnership

Response: After frankly discussing their conflicts in approach for a year, Ramon and his business partner decided to separate immediately and move ahead with new businesses; he immediately enjoyed the satisfaction of not being responsible to a partner.

Gerry

Change challenge: Dealing with a difficult business partner

Response: After carrying the burden of a draining business relationship for some years, she decided to end the partnership; she first worked to build up her emotional resilience and then reframed her thinking to change her career to teaching.

Carl and Elsa

Change challenge: Carl lost a job he had held for eleven years, then Elsa lost her job a year later.

Response: Carl tried to deal with his job loss without letting it be widely known, and Elsa assured him of her support; Elsa immediately reached out to a friend for support when she lost her job, and Carl made an effort to be a good listener.

Lessons:

- Working women often have another life of family and friends outside the job that gives them an advantage over men in coping with life changes.

- Women are more vulnerable to feeling inadequate with new and challenging assignments.
- Act as if you're succeeding.
- Take care of the "me" issues in a hurry.
- Set short-range goals and don't overpromise.
- During change, listen for adverse reaction and seek expert help.
- Practice flexibility, and build from your strengths.
- Create rituals for the small changes as well as the big ones.
- Acknowledge that saying goodbye is emotional.
- During change, communicate more often even though your instinct may be to clam up.
- Sometimes change requires that you learn to excel in the opposite gender's style.
- Men find it easier than women to discuss business problems frankly.
- Use people who love you as a sounding board for business problems.
- Changing times are a signal to look for ways to make your dreams happen.
- Understand that most partnerships have a natural ending and let it happen.
- Have the courage to break free. Much as we worry about bad things happening, it's the unexpected good things that most dramatically affect lives.
- Reach out to assure the other person of your love and support.

Life Situation 8: External Changes

Summary:
- In an unexpected change, the male approach is to grab the reins.

- Women will explore their options, negotiate, and try to avoid drastic consequences.

Examples:

Rosa and Dick

Change challenge: A casino being planned threatened to disrupt the economy and atmosphere of their rural community.

Response: They worked together to find ways to minimize the negative impact of the casino and use its arrival as an opportunity for local businesses; Dick stressed having a firm process in place for their plan and Rosa emphasized the incentives and motivations that would be necessary to add to it.

Joanne and Gene

Change challenge: School bus changes disrupted getting their children to the bus stop and Joanne to her job on time.

Response: Joanne reached out to the principal of the school her son went to and found that the bus schedule could be adjusted to get him to school.

Dominick and Mrs. Garcia

Change challenge: The year-long construction of a municipal building next door would disrupt the quiet life of Dominick and his mother as well as his ability to work at home.

Response: They renovated their home to have a higher, quieter floor; Dominick resolved to become more flexible and take up new activities such as tennis at the local Y; his mother became more involved in the nearest senior center.

Lessons:

- Develop your listening skills; women come by this more naturally, but everyone can improve by being aware of how he or she listens.

- Symbolize the response to change in a way that appeals both to men and women.
- Have a network of friends to call on for support in times of change.
- Remember to use your strengths to solve the problems that change brings.
- Act as if you'll have a positive outcome and you're more likely to have it.
- Reframe problem situations, by thinking like a child or, even better, listen to a child's view of your situation.
- Find a reframing buddy, and exercise your flexibility muscle.
- Break down big problems into smaller ones.

Index